THE
HOMEOWNERS
SURVIVAL GUIDE

THE HOMEOWNERS SURVIVAL GUIDE

Rosemary Burr

ROSTERS LTD, LONDON

Designed and published by ROSTERS LTD
Typeset by Busbys (The Printers) Ltd, Exeter
Printed and bound in Great Britain by Cox & Wyman Ltd, Reading
Previously published as Homeowners Guide
© Rosters Ltd 1988
Second edition 1991
ISBN 1-85631-012-7

CONTENTS

CHAPTER ONE:
CHOOSING YOUR HOME

Choosing a place to live is one of the most important decisions in our lives. A house is, after all, rather more than just a pile of bricks. Where you live can have a great effect on how you live and it is worth spending some time deciding just what you want – or rather what you can afford. These are the two crucial factors which need to be decided at the outset: location and price.

When looking for somewhere to buy you will probably have an idea of where you want to live. It may be within easy reach of your workplace or perhaps close to your children's school. It may be near relatives or in a part of the country you find particularly pleasant.

If you are retired you may move away from your present area. Perhaps for the first time in your life you will find yourself free to live virtually anywhere you want.

However, most of us do not have much choice when it comes to putting down roots. In general, those who are working will want to live within easy access of their workplace. Alternatively you may be prepared to commute to work, so that you can live outside the hurly burly of our inner cities. In this case you will have to take account of the costs of your daily journey to work when deciding where you are going to buy.

Setting your priorities

The first step is to define a rough area where you would like to move. It may be within a five mile radius of your work, a particular area of the country or a certain town. The next thing is to sort out how much money you can afford for your new home. This will probably be the chief constraint when you start treking around potential properties.

At the initial stage you only really need a rough estimate of how much you can afford. This will enable you to narrow your search and draw up a list of key requirements.

If you are a first time buyer you will need some money to put down as a deposit, usually around 10%. In pounds and pence, that's probably £7,500 in London and the South East and £5,000 elsewhere. If you have not got any savings, open a building society account immediately and start putting money away. Nothing impresses a mortgage lender quite as

9

much as some evidence that you can and do save. A good tip is to try and put aside every month the same amount of money that you can afford to spend on a mortgage. That way you will build up a substantial sum in a comparatively short time and you will show whoever you are approaching for a loan that you are a safe bet as a borrower.

A bank or building society will lend you money provided you are over eighteen and satisfy certain requirements. In general they want to see a proof of a steady income and a clean bill of health from anyone you have had financial dealings with in the past. This will include your bank, your landlord if you are renting, your employer and anyone who has lent you money.

Providing they are satisfied that you will be able to repay the loan they will consider lending you money around two and a half to three times your gross income. If you are married they will also take into account your spouse's income so that a rough guide would be two and a half times the larger income plus the spouse's income. Example: if you earn £9,000 a year and your spouse earns £7,500 then you could borrow two and a half times £9,000 which equals £22,500 plus £7,500 which totals £30,000. These are rough figures and individual lenders have different policies about how much they will lend. You may be able to borrow more but at this stage it is better to err on the side of caution.

EXAMPLES OF MORTGAGE REPAYMENTS			
Based on a 'repayment' mortgage, the figures show monthly repayments, net of basic tax at 25%, over a term of 25 years for various sized loans.			
NOMINAL INTEREST RATE: %	**£20,000**	**£30,000**	**£40,000**	**£50,000**
11.50	£164.56	£246.84	£342.28	£443.29
11.00	£159.48	£239.22	£331.11	£428.41
10.50	£154.48	£231.72	£320.08	£413.72
10.30	£152.50	£228.75	£315.72	£407.91
10.00	£149.52	£224.28	£309.22	£399.25
9.50	£144.64	£216.96	£298.53	£385.00
9.00	£139.82	£209.73	£288.01	£370.97

A GUIDELINE TO HOUSE PRICES ACROSS
THE UNITED KINGDOM FOR FIRST TIME BUYERS

REGION	One Bedroom Flat	Two Bedroom Flat	Two Bedroom Terraced House	TOTAL
Northern	22600.00	26879.03	27964.77	27516.67
Yorks & Humberside	29489.00	29775.00	31741.45	31471.45
North West	32912.95	48028.13	32632.14	33441.47
East Midlands	35596.89	37612.13	36059.06	36140.09
West Midlands	36433.33	41688.10	39703.03	39416.71
East Anglia	33435.68	41822.22	39734.45	38486.71
Outer South East	40016.85	45809.09	49482.22	46057.59
Outer Metropolitan	50889.21	56076.79	56586.00	54659.09
Greater London	55405.36	65992.85	69426.56	62437.17
South West	38439.83	44970.31	44711.63	43739.32
Wales	30662.50	34675.00	35457.00	34545.71
Scotland	27441.01	31587.57	34443.58	29288.08
Northern Ireland	*	*	25085.71	31511.11
TOTAL	41153.89	47989.71	42448.06	43093.82

Source: Business Analysis. Last quarter 1990.
* Insufficient sample.

Prices vary greatly according to area and location and therefore these examples should be read only as a guideline.

Having decided the maximum you can borrow, the next thing is to decide how much you can afford. The table shows how much you would need to pay each month on a repayment mortgage of £10,000, £15,000, £20,000 or £30,000 after you have received tax relief on the basis of seven different rates of interest. Remember, interest rates do fluctuate so leave yourself some room for any possible rises.

Now you know how much you can afford to borrow, in addition to the money you have already saved, you can go out and look for a property which suits your requirements and is in your price range. Prices for similar accommodation vary dramatically around the country with the South East being one of the more expensive regions. The table above shows prices for various types of property around the country at the start of 1988.

Second and third time buyers will already know the ropes. They must also take into account the amount of money they will get from the sale of their property. In general you subtract estate agent's fees, solicitor's, surveyor's and removal fees from the price you expect to get from your property to arrive at an estimate of how much you will have after the sale goes through. As a rough rule of thumb deduct 5%. After you have done that, you can calculate how much more you can afford to borrow in the same way as the first time buyer and add the two figures together.

What property?

Few countries in the world are as rich and diverse in the types of dwelling as may be found in the United Kingdom. It can and has been argued that the 'dwelling house', as the lawyers quaintly describe it, is the major achievement of architecture as practised in these isles. There are Devon thatched cottages, Northern back-to-backs, London terraces, high-rise tower blocks, Thirties semis and stately homes. However, the main distinction to keep in mind is between houses and flats.

Houses

Houses are generally sold freehold with vacant possession which means that you have, in effect, absolute ownership over the house and the land upon which it stands. In reality all land belongs to the Crown but to all intents and purposes if you own the freehold, then the property is yours.

Houses are either detached, semi-detached or terraced.

• Detached properties are more common in country areas and in the more expensive suburbs where houses stand in their own grounds. Semi-detached is the type of property which was built during the inter-war boom period. It was a way for builders to construct quite roomy houses and also save money as two houses share a common or party wall.

• Terraced housing mainly dates from the Georgian, Victorian and Edwardian eras. In fact, we owe the bulk of our existing terraced housing stock to the energetic house builders of pre-1919. Terraced housing can be the cheapest to buy.

• New houses don't fall neatly into any one category. They

may be terraced, semi-detached or detached. However, the fundamentals don't change. In general, terraced houses are the cheapest with semis and detached houses more expensive respectively.

Flats

Flats and maisonettes, that's the term for flats on two floors, are usually sold on long leases. This means that you do not own the property outright but you have exclusive rights to it for the term of the lease. You have to pay ground rent and maintenance charges. A typical long leasehold may be for ninety-nine years or more.

However, if you buy a leasehold you may find that part of the lease has already run. For example, there may be only seventy-eight years left to run out of the original ninety-nine. Some houses are also sold on long leases, although nationally this is less common.

Many first time buyers choose leasehold rather than freehold property. A two bedroom flat is probably more affordable than a three or four bedroom terraced or semi-detached house.

Flats may be either purpose built within a block or conversions of an older building, which might have been a large house. In the past few years a growing number of old redundant warehouses, factories and other working buildings have been converted into flats.

There is no hard and fast rule over which is better. Some conversions are excellent, while some purpose built flats are dreadful, and vice versa.

For and against

Houses Pros:
1. Houses have the advantage of generally being freehold which means that you do not have to pay ground rent to anyone, as you do with most leaseholds.
2. You do not have to rely on a landlord to repair or insure the property.
3. You do not have problems with neighbours living either above or below you.
4. Houses generally speaking are larger. They have more rooms and are likely to have a garden or at least a yard.

Houses Cons:
1. Cost. Houses are usually more expensive to buy.
2. Houses require more maintenance and, as the freeholder, you have sole responsibility for their upkeep.
3. They are more expensive to run with higher electricity and heating bills.
4. The rates are usually higher than flats per square footage.

Flats Pros:
1. They are comparatively cheap to buy.
2. They are often physically smaller, too, which may suit a single person or couple who do not need a lot of space.
3. They may require less maintenance or the maintenance might be the responsibility of the landlord.
4. They will usually be less trouble to look after than a house and bills will be smaller.

Flats Cons:
1. They may be too small for your requirements.
2. You may be disturbed by noise from your upstairs or downstairs neighbours.
3. Your landlord may not be too careful about fulfilling the obligations concerning the repair and upkeep of the property, the insurance of the buildings and the cleaning and maintenance of any common parts.
4. Restrictions within the lease may limit your total freedom to do as you wish in your property.

Making your choice

The type of property you choose will be determined partly by how much you want to spend. In London, for example, few first time buyers can now afford to buy a freehold house and will have to settle for a flat for the time being, usually a conversion of a terraced house.

In other parts of the country, particularly the North or the Midlands, property prices are so low that few people are interested in flats unless they have special features. It will also depend on how you want to live. Elderly and retired people, for example, may not want the trouble of looking after a large house and garden. Now, their needs are being catered for by the increased provision of specialist sheltered housing.

Similarly, a young single professional person or couple may want an apartment which is relatively maintenance-free. This will give them time to get on which their careers and their social lives, unencumbered with chores like having to mow the lawn.

The third factor is, of course, location. In some parts of the country your choice will be limited to the type of property that is readily available. In Edinburgh, for example, there are very few freehold houses and what few there are available are consequently very expensive. In the country, you are unlikely to find many semi-detached or terraced houses.

Starting the hunt

You know what you want to buy and how much you can afford, so now's the time to take the plunge. The vast majority of homes in this country are still sold by those men and women we all love to hate, the estate agents. Remember it is their job to sell you a home, they are acting for the seller, not you. They earn their money from the cash you pay to buy a property on their books.

The best bet is to try and draw up a short list of agents who specialise in the area where you wish to buy. Try checking the local hoardings, particularly in London, and papers for names. Then make a personal visit, establish contact and go through the various information sheets there and then in the agent's office. This will show you are serious and help weed out the no-hopers from the start. Have a good chat with the agent, a good agent can save your shoe leather and petrol, but you do need to be able to say in fairly strict terms exactly what you are looking for. An agent can't help if he or she doesn't know what you want.

Another route is to drop into your local property shop, if there is one. The choice might not be so great, but it's worth a quick trip. You can also try scanning the local papers, often a good source of bargains and quickie deals. The national Sundays also have property columns, which are worth keeping an eye out for.

What to look for

Once you have made up your mind about location, price

range and style of accommodation you want, the great house hunting trail begins in earnest. Assuming from the written particulars that a property meets your broad criteria the next thing to do is go and look at it.

It is essential that you look around a property in daylight. Apart from the fact that you can literally see more, you will get a much clearer impression of the property in the full glare of day. Never commit yourself one way or the other without seeing the place during the day. Ideally you should try to pick a cloudy day – not too difficult in the British climate – for an authentic feel.

You will also get a much clearer picture of the property's surroundings during the day. For example, you may not have noticed the bottle crushing factory next door if you went around in the evening, or the view over the London to Norwich express railway line. Conversely, if you have only seen the property during the day try and look around in the evening. You may find that the traffic noise is more noticeable than you originally thought or discover that the pop group next door practices into the early hours of the morning.

Property check-up

If you decide that you are interested in a particular property then a cool, clear and objective appraisal at this stage can save you a lot of money later on.

(a) Houses

The age of the property is one of the most important factors to consider when looking at houses. Older houses are prone to a number of faults such as rising damp, leaking roofs, dry rot, damaged, rotting or infested woodwork. They may also have suffered from some unusual or unorthodox 'improvements' or 'conversions' in the past, which may need substantial work to sort out.

Start with the outside of the property. Is it in disrepair or does it give the impression of being well-maintained? Is the woodwork sound and the brickwork in good condition? Poor brickwork in an older property is one of the more expensive jobs to put right. Often the mortar has crumbled requiring the brickwork to be repointed or rendered over.

Are any of the walls slanting or bulging outwards? Are there any suspicious cracks that might indicate subsidence? In older properties this often occurs where the ground on which the house stands has shifted perhaps due to drying out over the years. The bad drought in 1976, for example, caused many problems of this nature, particularly in areas of clay bearing sub-soil.

Are the gutters and downspouts in good condition and are the drains working adequately? If you can see the roof, are there any slates or coping stones or ridge tiles missing? Are the chimney stacks straight and the chimney pots in good condition? A pair of field glasses is useful for this type of external examination. Is the brickwork and the cement rendering sound?

Turning to the inside of the property, is it in reasonable repair and decoration? Does the room lay-out suit your needs or will you need to do any building work? Are the services, water, gas, electricity, working or do they need repair or replacement? If the property has lead piping for the water, iron pipes for the gas and round pin plug sockets for the electricity, then the chances are that the whole lot needs to be replaced.

Is there any indication of damp, dry rot or woodworm? Damp can be spotted by telltale signs such as peeling or discoloured wallpaper, crumbling plasterwork, crystallisation of salts out of the plaster, or a musty odour. It may be due to rising damp, because the damp proof course has failed, because earth is piled up against the exterior of the building, or because ventilation holes have become blocked. Dry rot can be spotted by cracked woodwork where the cracks go across the grain of the wood. In bad cases there may be signs of the fungus itself. Woodworm can be spotted by the tiny holes that the lavae make in eating their way through the timber.

Does the owner have damp-proof and timber guarantees? Is there any discoloration of the upstairs ceilings which might indicate that the roof is leaking? If you can, get into the roof space and see if there is any daylight showing through the tiles and felt, that is if the roof has been felted. If it has not, then it will probably need a roof overhaul.

If there have been any major alterations or additions to

the structure of the house such as a loft conversion, extension or other major structural improvement, ask whether the owner sought planning consent or building regulations approval. Many people do work on their homes which may be illegal if carried out without planning permission. If the worst comes to the worst, the local authority might force you to take down the illegal structure. If you suspect that work has been carried out without planning permission, consult the local authority planning department or a surveyor.

Is the house of a conventional construction? This means brick and thermal blocks in most cases with a slate, concrete, clay or asbestos tiled roof. Older houses will be either brick or stone construction, while more modern houses will be basically thermal blocks with an exterior facing of brick.

Some older properties might have an unusual construction such as Tudor or mediaeval timber frame with wattle and daub infill, thatched roofs or cob walls (basically rubble with an outer skin of rendering).

Professional advice should be sought with unusual types of construction as mortgage lenders have different attitudes when it comes to these types of building. Insurance costs for unusual constructions, thatch being the worst culprit, can be twice as high as for conventional property.

New houses have their share of problems. Check for ill-fitting windows, warped door frames, rough plasterwork and signs of settlement. This can occur in new properties where the house has been built on an ill-prepared site or one which has recently been filled in and is still in the process of settling down.

If you are buying a new house you should ask to see the NHBC certificate which comes with the property. This is a ten year guarantee that covers virtually all defects to the property in the first two years after it has been built and any major structural defects for the remaining eight years.

If the house has just been built, the builder or developer should provide an NHBC certificate within a couple of months of completing the property. Nearly all new homes are covered by the NHBC scheme. If the house you are looking at is not, then you should ask why. Most mortgage lenders will not lend money on a new house which is not covered.

A new rival scheme to the NHBC scheme called Muniguard

is being introduced. However, some mortgage lenders are waiting to see how the scheme works in practice before lending on properties carrying this new guarantee. Many new homes are still built using timber frame construction methods. Despite the furore that has surrounded this method in the past there is no evidence that it is a better or worse form of construction than conventional brick and block. However, it is different and timber frame homes cannot be treated in the same way as brick ones.

Greater care has to be taken when knocking holes through the walls, for example, so that the thermal insulation and damp proofing are not damaged. Wall fixings are different, too, and professional advice should be taken before making any major alterations to the structure of the building. Timber frame's advantages lie in its good insulating properties for both heat and sound so there is no need to install cavity insulation. Indeed, this can be harmful. Virtually all mortgage lenders make no distinction between brick, block and timber frame when they consider making a loan.

Flats

Many of the points concerning the structure of the property apply whether you are considering a house, flat, or a maisonette. An examination of the exterior of the building is important, but remember that the repair and maintenance of the building will be the responsibility of either the landlord or the leaseholders. The general state of repair will tell you a lot about the relationship between leaseholders and landlord, or the ability of the leaseholders to effect their own repairs.

Check on the access to the flat that you are considering. Are the stairs, hallways and common parts maintained properly? These again will be either the responsibility of the landlord or the joint responsibility of the leaseholders.

Ask whether there are any major repairs outstanding. While it may be the landlord's responsibility to make sure the property is in good repair, it will be your money as a leaseholder that will pay for it.

Many flat buyers have purchased a property only to find

that they are landed with a major repairs bill as soon as they have moved in.

In many new flats or leasehold properties, the freehold will be owned by a management company and all of the leaseholders will have a share in it. Such 'condominium' arrangements, popular in the USA, are becoming increasingly common here in the UK as a way to avoid the freehold remaining in the hands of an outside landlord.

Check the length of the lease. If a lease is coming towards the end of its life, then it can affect the value of the property. Many mortgage lenders insist that the lease must run at least fifteen or twenty years longer than the term of the mortgage loan. This means that on a typical mortgage loan over twenty-five years the lender will insist on a lease with forty or forty-five years left to run.

If you are buying a flat in England or Wales avoid freehold flats, sometimes called flying freeholds. The main problem with these is that there is no landlord who you can turn to when the common parts and exterior of the building need attention or general maintenance. In addition, there may be problems agreeing a general set of rules with the other freeholders over such things as double glazing, altering the windows and the building's exterior.

Check with other flat residents to make sure the landlord fulfills his duties to their satisfaction. Remember the seller of the property is not obliged to tell you anything. It may be that the landlord, or the managing agents acting for the landlord, do not do their job properly or charge exorbitant rates for repairs or insurance. New flats will be covered by the NHBC certificate in the same way as new houses are.

If you do decide to proceed with a particular purchase ask your solicitor to check the lease and tell you which common parts you are responsible for helping to maintain. In some leases, the roof, which can be particularly problematic and expensive to repair, is not the responsibility of flat residents.

Buying council property

Under the government's 'Right to Buy' legislation – first introduced in 1980 – tenants of council homes, houses, flats and maisonettes rented from housing associations have the right to buy their home from the landlord after two years tenancy. In order to encourage sales, the government offers substantial discounts to buyers. These start at 32% after two year's tenancy for houses increasing by 1% for every additional year that you have been a tenant of the public sector landlord. The maximum discount is 60% after thirty years. For flats the discount scale runs from 44% after two years tenancy increasing by 2% for every extra year that you are a tenant. The maximum here is a massive 70 per cent discount after fifteen years. The discount is subject to a financial ceiling of £25,000, although this figure is under review. If the property is resold within three years of purchase then a proportion of the discount has to be repaid.

Tenants exercising their right to buy flats or maisonnettes have extra protection against unexpected service charges levied by the landlord. Before the sale, the landlord of flats and maisonettes must give binding estimates of service charges for repairs to be carried out during the first five years of the lease. Under the legislation, the landlord is obliged to ensure that mortgage finance is provided for 'Right to Buy' sales subject of course to the buyer meeting the lender's criteria. Local authorities used to provide loans themselves, but they now usually channel mortgage applicants to building societies or specialist mortgage lenders.

Buying at auction

Instead of selling a house in the normal way, more and more people are auctioning their property. Buying and selling for that matter, at auction has distinct advantages although it is not without its drawbacks as well. As a buyer you can pick up some bargains at auction. The seller will have his or her reasons for going to an auction, usually because a quick sale is sought. This often, but not always, means buyers benefit from a very competitive price for the property.

At auction the seller will have stipulated a minimum price he or she wants for the property – the so-called 'reserve price'. If bids fail to reach this figure then the property will be withdrawn from sale. If, however, your bid is over the reserve and is the highest offer, then the sale is concluded at the time when the auctioneer's hammer hits the table. After the auction you will be required to pay a deposit of 10% of the sale price with the balance to follow – usually four weeks later.

From this you will gather that it is vital that you have had the survey, valuation and mortgage arranged before the auction. Of course, there is a risk any expenses you ran up before the auction for surveys etc. may be wasted if someone else puts in a higher bid. It is vital that you sort your finances out before going to the auction. There is no point in bidding for a property, only to find that you cannot get a mortgage on it, or that the potential lender's valuation of the property is way below the price you agreed to pay.

So remember to have the property valued before the auction and also try to obtain initial approval from a lender for a mortage on the property. In the past building societies and banks used to be very chary about promising mortgages to people buying at auction. However, many lenders adopt a more flexible line these days.

Once you have had a valuation on the property, decide how much you are prepared to pay for it. Once you have made up your mind how much the property is worth – stick to it. Do not go above your own figure just because someone else is prepared to pay more.

Remember, there will be other properties and other days. So be prepared to let this one go if the bidding goes higher than your target price.

Don't forget you'll need to pay the deposit immediately. So make sure you have the money or at least have agreed bridging finance *in advance*.

Surveys

While a first hand inspection of the property that you are interested in is a good start, you should think about having a survey conducted by a professional surveyor.

The mortgage lender will invariably have a valuation survey done on the property before they will lend money on it. Usually they will let you have a copy of this survey if you ask for it.

However, the mortgage lender's interest is in ensuring that the property is sound enough to lend money on and that, in the last resort, the lender can always get their money back. A valuation report is not a full survey and if you want a professional opinion about the property you will have to pay for your own survey to be carried out.

Most mortgage lenders now offer a House Buyer's Report and Valuation. This is a fuller appraisal of the property by the surveyor who is carrying out the mortgage valuation and report.

By combining the two functions in one visit – valuation and survey – costs are kept down. The surveyor fills out a standard form which provides information about the state of the dwelling. A more comprehensive report on the property is provided by a full structural survey.

For this the surveyor will be acting exclusively for you and will provide a full and comprehensive report on the state of the building. However, this is necessarily more expensive. A House Buyer's Report may typically cost around £120 to £150 while a full structural survey will cost upwards of £200.

If you are in any doubt about the state of the property or you do not have sufficient knowledge yourself to form a judgement then a survey is advisable. In most cases the House Buyer's Report will be sufficient to uncover any major problems that the property might be concealing.

Checklist

1. **Fix your requirements**
   Decide where you want to live, how much you can afford and the type of property you want, e.g. house (detached, semi, terraced) flat or maisonette.

2. **Arrange finance**
   Get verbal and, if possible, written commitment from the lender for the mortgage loan. Make sure you have access to sufficient cash for a 10% deposit. If not open a savings account immediately or go to your bank to arrange a loan. You could also try your building society which since 1987 has been permitted to make unsecured loans, although only a few have taken up the option under the new law.

3. If you are buying new property

Check that the builder has registered the property with the NHBC and that NHBC insurance cover will be issued.

4. If you are buying a house

Do you need a survey? If you are unhappy about some aspects of the property or feel that you do not have the knowledge to form a judgement then ask a surveyor to report on it for you. Don't rely on the mortgage lender's valuation. This is really intended to ensure that the property is adequate security for the loan. For a fuller report, instruct your own surveyor or ask your mortgage lender for a House Buyer's Report.

While you are looking around the property initially check:

(a) exterior brickwork, pointing, guttering, downspouts, roof and chimneys, window frames.

(b) interior for rising and penetrating damp, dry rot, woodworm.

(c) damp proof and timber treatment guarantees or reports.

(d) water, gas and electricity services to see if they need replacing, central heating if any.

(e) any unusual additions, extensions or structural changes to the house. Ask the seller of the property if planning permission or building regulation clearance was needed and sought from the local authority.

5. If you are buying a flat, check:

(a) that the landlord or management company are fulfilling their obligations, that there are no outstanding repairs on the property or if so how much they are going to cost.

(b) that the lease has long enough left to run. At least 20 years longer than the term of your mortgage loan.

(c) that common parts (stairs, hallways, lifts, etc.) are cleaned and maintained to the leaseholder's satisfaction.

(d) that the buildings are adequately insured and that the landlord is not overcharging.

6. Make sure that the property suits your needs, check:

(a) that the number and layout of the rooms and the size of the garden, if any, are suitable for your present needs and for the foreseeable future.

(b) that the house gets adequate sunlight. A house which faces due north or east is going to get less sun than one that faces south or west.

(c) that you do not have to share a driveway with your neighbour, that the boundaries of the property are clearly marked.

(d) that the neighbours and the street are reasonably quiet and that it is not near a factory which is noisy or smelly.

(e) that there are no major building works or road schemes planned for the area that you do not know of.

7. How much will it cost you? Check:

(a) the monthly repayments on the mortgage, how much you pay in rates, what are the monthly bills.

(b) on a leasehold property find out the cost of the annual ground rent, any service costs, buildings insurance.

CHAPTER TWO:
ARRANGING THE FINANCE

Few of us are fortunate enough to buy our home outright and so we rely on a mortgage to make up the difference between the cash we have and the price of the house we wish to buy. A mortgage is simply a loan which is secured against the property that you are buying. In other words, the lender knows that they can get their money back by selling your home and using the proceeds to repay the original loan.

Before you start looking for a home you can ask your building society or bank to give you some idea of how much they would be prepared to lend, assuming, of course, that the property you choose meets with their approval. How does the building society or bank decide how much it will lend you? Basically, they look at two facts. How much you earn and how much they think you can repay. These are not the same thing.

Borrowing capacity

First, they will want to know how much you earn per year. Generally speaking they will then lend you a certain multiple of that figure. These status calculations, or earnings multiples as they are sometimes called, vary from lender to lender. In addition, if you are taking out a joint mortgage the lender will usually take into account the second income.

Assessing your ability to repay is another matter and far from simple. The building society branch manager or bank manager who is dealing with your application will exercise his or her discretion and experience at this stage. He or she will consider not just your current income, but prospects for the future. Overtime, if included, must be consistent as must any earnings from part-time work. If your income is made up partly or largely from commissions you will be asked to show how this level can be maintained. Similarly if you are self-employed the building society or bank will want to go over your trading prospects. Some lenders may take into account the number and age of your dependants, your hire purchase commitments and any other large outstanding debts when making their assessment.

When you apply for a mortgage, make sure that your financial affairs are in order. It's probably more important to show you can manage your money and handle loan

27

repayments than simply to earn a reasonable salary. So, if for example you have borrowed money in the past and repaid it on time, take along the paperwork as proof. You should also take copies of your bank statements and any evidence you have of regular savings. You will then be in a better position to show that you are the type of person who is able to handle the mortgage repayments. If you are a first time buyer who has been renting, take along your rent book to show that you have paid your rent regularly and are not in arrears.

Once you know in general terms how much you can borrow, you can then go out and look for a property. Remember, though, that a bank or building society will in normal circumstances only lend you up to 80% of the value of the property, not the price that is being asked. This means that you will have to find the remainder of the money yourself. For first time buyers who cannot afford to pay 20% of the purchase price mortgage lenders will occasionally lend up to 95% or even 100% of the value of the property.

The portion of your mortgage over 80% is usually guaranteed by an insurance company and you will be asked to pay a one-off premium for this additional policy. The insurance premium is calculated on the basis of a certain percentage of the amount of the loan which is to be guaranteed. For example, in Autumn 1990 a typical fee was 7% of the sum guaranteed. On a mortgage of £60,000 representing 100% of the property's value, a lender would normally advance £48,000, i.e. 80%. The remaining 20% would be guaranteed by an insurance policy which would cost 9.7% of £12,000, i.e. £840. Most building societies impose a ceiling on the cost of the property for which they are prepared to lend 100%.

The lender will only make a loan on the basis of how much the property is worth – not on what you are prepared to pay for it. A house on the market for £60,000, for example, may only be valued by the lender's valuer at £55,000. If so, it is this lower figure that will be used when calculating 80%.

Choosing your mortgage

When you apply for a mortgage you will be asked which type you want, so it is very important that you understand the options available. Don't be confused by the vast array of different product names – under the fancy packaging, most are variants of these two basic types of mortgage, repayment or endowment.

Repayment mortgage

A repayment mortgage is the simplest option. The lender advances you the money and you repay the loan over a period of time which is agreed at the outset. Most people opt for twenty-five years but loans can be repaid over a number of years ranging usually between five and twenty-five, depending on the age of the borrower, the size of the loan and your ability to repay. In rare circumstances thirty-year loans can be arranged. Interest is normally added to the outstanding amount of the loan to be repaid every twelve months.

In the early years of a repayment loan, most of the monthly payments will be interest, with only a small amount going to reduce the size of the loan itself. In the later years the situation is reversed. The monthly payments will be largely reducing the debt with only a small amount of interest. Tax relief is given to UK resident taxpayers on interest payments on mortgages for their main home of up to £30,000. There is no tax relief on capital repayments.

A number of lenders will insist that you take out insurance cover on your life so that if anything happens to you as the main breadwinner, the mortgage may be repaid. Full details of this are given in Chapter Five. Generally speaking repayment mortgages are simple, flexible and can usually be tailored to meet your changing financial circumstances. Some lenders used to charge a penalty for early repayment, but this practice is now dying out.

Endowment mortgages

The second common way of repaying a mortgage is through an endowment mortgage. Its more correct title is an endowment linked mortgage. Here's how it works. Instead of repaying capital and interest every month, so that the outstanding amount of the loan reduces gradually, your monthly instalments cover interest on the loan and a separate premium payment on an endowment policy with an insurance company. An endowment policy is a type of savings scheme which also incorporates life insurance. The insurance company invests your money and at the end of the mortgage term you receive the proceeds of the endowment policy. This is used to repay the original mortgage loan and any money left over comes to you as a tax-free lump sum. If the proceeds are not sufficient to repay the loan you will need to come up with the difference.

If you want to buy another property you may be able to simply reassign the policy. You may need to take out another policy if the second home is more expensive than the first. Alternatively you may decide to cash in the policy. Its value will depend upon the insurance company's investment performance and its so-called surrender policy. In the first few years, you may get a poor return on your premiums paid. Remember endowment policies should be considered as a long term commitment and the value of investments can fall as well as rise.

On the plus side, with an endowment linked mortgage you have the chance to build up a tax-free lump sum which you can spend as you choose once your policy is mature. It also includes sufficient life cover so that if you die the mortgage will be repaid.

Pension mortgage

In essence, the pension mortgage is similar to an endowment mortgage. A pension mortgage is paid off by the proceeds from a personal pension plan, remembering, of course, that the value of your pension plan will reflect the value of the investments held and that these may increase or decrease in value. You opt to receive a smaller pension and use the tax-free lump sum to repay the mortgage. If pension policy is used in this way, there is less pension on retirement. Some people take out a pension policy and endowment policy to get over this.

Pension mortgages are very tax efficient but rather inflexible. Your pension plan contributions, up the statutory limits, qualify for tax relief. So, if you pay tax at 40% you will qualify for tax relief on your contributions at 40%. The money inside the pension plan itself grows tax-free. So assuming the same investment policy over the same timespan, you'll earn more on your money in a pension policy than in an endowment policy.

Another thing to consider with pension mortgages at the moment is that if you subsequently join a company which has its own pension scheme which you wish to join then your existing plan will have to become what is called 'paid-up'. This means you cannot continue to contribute to it and you will be unlikely to have sufficient money to repay your mortgage if you have recently taken out the loan. If this happens you'll need to start an endowment policy to cover the mortgage. Depending on your age, this can work out rather expensive. However, under new rules introduced in April 1988, employers can no longer make membership of the company pension scheme a condition of employment and so this problem will largely disappear.

Other varieties of mortgage

Apart from the two staple types of mortgage, there are a number of variations which are marketed by building societies, banks and specialist lending institutions. These include:

● Constant net basis (sometimes called net rate annuity)
Under this system, as its name suggests, your monthly repayments are fixed in advance. They are calculated simply by applying the net interest rate, i.e. after tax relief has been granted, to the loan. The advantages are the security of knowing how much your monthly bill will be, provided interest rates remain the same, and being able to spread the tax relief more evenly through the life of the loan.

● Varying repayment (gross profile)
This is calculated on the basis of first working out the net

monthly payment and then applying tax relief only to the interest portion. In the early years, the interest component is higher than the capital, which means after taking account of tax relief the net monthly payments start low and gradually rise to reflect the declining proportion of interest as against capital. Under this system you pay off the loan more slowly than under the constant net basis and your monthly payments increase each year. If inflation is rising rapidly or your income increasing fast then you may prefer a system which starts with lower monthly payments and then involves higher payments later on.

MORTGAGE INTEREST RELIEF AT SOURCE (MIRAS)

Examples: £10,000 loan
25 year term

Gross Interest Rate	11%
Basic Rate of Tax	29%
Net Interest Rate After Tax Relief	7.81% (i.e. 11.00 × 71%)

(A) CONSTANT NET BASIS – NET RATE ANNUITY

YEAR 1   £

Monthly payments at net rate of interest = £76.80	
Annual payment = £76.80 × 12 =	921.60
Less: Interest at 7.81% on £10,000	781.00
Capital repaid in year	140.60

YEAR 2

Monthly payments as above again give annual payment of	921.60
Interest at 7.81% on £9,859.40 (£10,000 − £140.60)	770.01
Capital repaid in year	151.59

YEAR 3

Monthly payments as above again give annual payment of	921.60
Interest at 7.81% on £9,707.81 (£9,859.40 − £151.59)	758.17
Capital repaid in year	163.43

YEAR 4

Opening balance £9,544.38 – Total capital of £455.62 having been repaid.

(B) VARYING REPAYMENT – GROSS PROFILE
YEAR 1

Monthly payment at 11.00% (N.B. gross rate of interest) – £98.95 of which £91.67 (£10,000 × 11.00% divided by 12) is interest and therefore £7.28 capital. If borrower is permitted to deduct basic tax relief on interest charged on £91.67 then tax relief is £26.58 (£91.67 × 29%)

Borrower's net monthly payment (Reduced Amount) this year is £98.95 − £26.58 =	**£72.37**

The account for the year results viz:

Total annual payment £72.37 × 12 =	868.44
Interest charged at 7.81% on £10,000	781.00
Capital repaid in year	87.44

YEAR 2

Opening balance now £10,000 − £87.44 =	9,912.56

Gross monthly payment as before £98.95 of which this year £90.87 (£9,912.56 × 11.00% divided by 12) is interest and £8.08 is capital. If borrower is permitted to deduct basic tax relief on interest charged on £90.87 then tax relief per month this year is £26.35 (£90.87 × 29%)

Borrower's net monthly payment (Reduced Amount) this year is therefore £98.95 − £26.35 =	72.60

The account for the year results viz:

Total annual payment £72.60 × 12	871.20
Interest charged @ 7.81% on £9,912.56 =	774.17
Capital repaid this year	97.03

YEAR 3

Opening balance now £9,912.56 − £97.03 =	£9,815.53

Gross monthly payment as before £98.95 of which this year £89.98 (£9,815.53 × 11.00% divided by 12) is interest and £8.97 is capital. If borrower is permitted to deduct basic tax relief on interest charged of £89.98 then tax relief is £26.09 (£89.98 × 29%)

Borrower's net monthly repayment (Reduced Amount) this year is therefore £98.95 − £26.09) =	72.86

The account for the year results viz:

Total annual payment £72.86 × 12 =	874.32
Interest charged @ 7.81% on £9,815.53 =	766.59
Capital repaid this year	107.73

YEAR 4

Opening balance £9,707.80 (£9,815.53 − £107.73) Total capital of £292.20 having been repaid.

CONCLUSION

	Under Constant Net Basis	Under Varying Repayment Basis
(a)	After 3 years capital of £455.62 has been repaid	After 3 years £292.20 has been repaid
(b)	Payments will continue at £76.20 per month	The monthly payment increases each year

Source: The Nationwide Anglia Building Society

Low start mortgages

Buyers on low incomes and first time buyers may need a little extra assistance to get on the house buying ladder. A low start mortgage can help where a buyer does not have sufficient income to take out a big enough loan but whose income will grow in the next few years.

Low start mortgages usually involve some form of subsidy for the repayments in the initial years of the mortgage to enable the borrower to take on a larger loan than he or she would otherwise be able to afford.

There are two common ways of doing this, either by using part or all of the deposit on the property to subsidise the monthly repayments over the first few years or by deferring any repayment of capital in the first year or two of the mortgage so that the borrower is only paying interest. The capital is 'rolled up' over the remaining years of the mortgage.

Some schemes may involve a reduced rate of interest in the first years of the mortgage with the balance of the interest being added to the outstanding mortgage and interest charged on the whole lot.

All these schemes have the common purpose of reducing initial outgoings. However, the borrower does eventually pay through higher repayments over the remainder of the mortgage term. If the mortgage is taken out for twenty-five or thirty years, however, these increased costs can be negligible.

Low-cost endowments

A low cost endowment is a variation of the endowment mortgage in which the premiums of the insurance policy taken out to repay the mortgage loan are kept as low as possible. In a conventional endowment mortgage, the policy will usually incorporate some element of guarantee that it will produce a certain return. The insurance company will point out that the eventual sum paid out will be higher because it will declare profits every year and allocate bonuses to the policy.

For a low cost endowment the assumption is made that the insurance company will invest your money at a sufficient profit so that a smaller endowment than would otherwise be necessary can be taken out. The difference between the projected benefit for the endowment policy and the mortgage, which will eventually be repaid, will be covered by the profits generated by the policy.

Although the probability is that the insurance company's profits will be more than adequate to repay the mortgage, there is always the risk that they will not. In that case, you would have to pay the difference from your own pocket. If the policy produces a surplus over and above what is needed to repay the mortgage loan then you would keep the difference.

Low cost endowments have become more popular since the withdrawal of tax relief on insurance premiums, as falling interest rates have made full endowment policies less attractive for many basic rate taxpayers than ordinary repayment mortgages. The insurance companies have recently been warned by the authorities not to make over-optimistic estimates of the returns on their policies in case these cannot be fulfilled.

Unit-linked mortgages

Another form of endowment mortgage uses a unit-linked insurance policy to repay the mortgage loan. Unlike a conventional 'with-profits' endowment policy, the insurance company offers no guarantee that the policy will provide a particular sum after so many years. Instead the policy offers investment in unitised funds which may or may not produce a much better return than the conventional policy. However, because the investments are directly linked to the fortunes of the stock market, the value of the money invested in units goes up and down. If the underlying investments perform well, then the policyholder gets the benefit. If they perform badly, then the policyholder has to take the brunt of the loss. Policyholders give up the guarantee of a certain return on their money in the hope that their investments will perform much better – and in the long run over the past fifteen years the best unit-linked policies have out-performed the best with-profits. However, this is largely because of the rapid rise in international stock market prices in the past few years.

Do remember that the short term fluctuations of the underlying investments in a unit-linked policy mean that it may be worth a lot more today than it is worth next week or next year. Over the longer term the policy will probably easily pay off the mortgage and provide a handsome profit for the policyholder as well. There is the possibility, however, that the underlying investments will fall in value and a unit-linked policy offers no safety net. Policyholders just have to stand the loss. For this reason, some mortgage lenders will not accept unit-linked endowment policies to repay mortgage loans although, in general, they are becoming more widely acceptable.

Fixed rate mortgages

Instead of the mortgage interest rate varying according to the levels of general rates, you can take out a loan at a rate which is fixed for a certain period of time. If the average current mortgage rate is 12%, for example, then a bank or other lender might offer a fixed rate loan at 11% for three years.

This may seem attractive but remember it is rather a gamble. If rates fall sharply, everyone else may be paying 10% while you are stuck at 11%.

The chief advantage of the fixed rate loan is that you know how much you are going to pay each month for the period over which the rate is fixed. Some fixed rate loans have an option at the end of the original period to convert into another fixed rate loan at terms set by the lender. Otherwise, the loan normally reverts to the standard mortgage rate, with fluctuating payments depending on the current level of interest rates.

During 1990 high interest rates in the UK made fixed rate mortgages relatively popular. However, there was still a limited supply.

Shared ownership

Shared ownership is a scheme introduced through the Housing Corporation and housing associations to enable people who cannot afford to buy a home outright to buy at least part of it. The scheme allows buyers to purchase a proportion of the equity of the property and pay rent on the remainder.

The schemes are offered through housing associations and differ slightly from one association to another. In general all of the schemes work in a similar way. The property is valued by a qualified valuer and the buyer can buy a proportion of the equity of the property, starting at 25%.

The housing association which is running the scheme then charges rent on the remaining portion of the equity of the property that the buyer has not bought. Recent changes to the law allow housing associations to charge market rents for the rented part of shared ownership leases and this should increase the attractiveness and availability of such schemes.

The buyer can subsequently buy the remainder of the equity in the property in stages. Usually this will be 25%, 50% or 75% until you own the property outright. If you prefer, you can continue to pay rent on the portion of the property you do not own without having to buy the remainder.

Mortgage finance for the share in the property bought can be arranged in the usual way. Further details of the shared ownership scheme can be obtained from regional offices of the Housing Corporation who will also be able to provide details of housing associations offering the scheme in your area. Your local Citizens' Advice Bureau or local authority will be able to provide the address of your regional office.

Taking your pick

One of the greatest areas of disagreement in personal finance is the best type of mortgage to recommend. Before March 1984, when life assurance premium relief was abolished on assurance plans, the pro-endowment linked camp were in the majority. Now the case is much less clear cut and depends upon your age, the length of the loan and, often crucially, the level of interest rates. Since one thing we know for sure is that we do not know what interest rates will be in the future, it is impossible to make any hard and fast calculations.

In general it is best to ask for estimates for a variety of types of mortgages and see whether you can afford the monthly repayments. It is very difficult to compare the relative value for money as an endowment linked policy's ultimate value will depend upon the insurance company's investment ability and the general level of stock market prices around the world. The table on page 38 shows the comparative costs of the three basic types of mortgage, assuming a £20,000 loan repayable over twenty-five years. The insurance premiums shown are a guide and will depend on the insurance company used, your age, health and sex. The illustrations are based on a joint life endowment policy and mortgage protection policy but other alternatives are available. Always ask for up-to-date quotations from your lender.

Tax

Interest on a mortgage loan of up to £30,000 to buy your own home qualifies for tax relief. This relief is given at your marginal rate of tax, so is worth more to a higher rate taxpayer than someone paying basic rate tax. For example, if you pay tax at 40% you will qualify for tax relief of up to 40% on part or all of your mortgage, depending upon its size. From August 1988 the £30,000 limit will apply to the property regardless of the number of borrowers.

Most of us pay tax at the basic rate which is currently 25%. In 1983 the Inland Revenue introduced a new scheme for giving basic tax relief on mortgage interest at source (MIRAS). MIRAS is the way in which you obtain tax relief at the basic rate on your mortgage repayments without having to lift a finger. Gone are the days when you needed to apply to the tax office and wait until they amended your tax coding.

Mortgages up to £30,000 usually come into the MIRAS scheme provided they are arranged through a recognised lender. This covers most banks and building societies. The

MORTGAGE REPAYMENT COMPARISON TABLES

The tables below illustrate the total monthly cost of a mortgage on repayment, low-cost endowment and pension schemes. They are based on a £30,000 loan over 25 years for a male aged 35 next birthday and a female aged 32 next birthday, assuming they are basic rate (25%) tax payers. Low-cost endowment and pension mortgages aim to provide a surplus at the end of the agreement, as well as paying off the mortgage sum. However there is no guarantee that these policies will produce a favourable return – their value can go down as well as up and it is even conceivable that the fund produced at the end of the term would not be enough to pay off the mortgage.

TYPE OF MORTGAGE	INTEREST RATE 11% (8.25% NET)			INTEREST RATE 10.30% (7.725% NET)			INTEREST RATE 9.50% (7.125% NET)		
	Monthly payment	Assurance premium	Total monthly cost	Monthly payment	Assurance premium	Total monthly cost	Monthly payment	Assurance premium	Total monthly cost
REPAYMENT	239.22	14.00	253.22	228.72	14.00	242.72	216.95	14.00	230.95
LOW-COST ENDOWMENT	206.25	41.90	248.15	193.12	41.90	235.02	178.12	41.90	220.02
PENSION	206.25	39.12	245.37	193.12	39.12	232.25	178.12	39.12	217.25

lender then charges you an interest rate which is net of basic rate tax. So, for example, if the gross payments on an endowment mortgage are £200, the lender will charge under the MIRAS scheme a net figure of £150.

Tax relief is only given on the interest component of your monthly repayment, not the capital. If the mortgage on your home is for more than £30,000 then you will only qualify for tax relief on interest payments on up to £30,000 under the current tax rules. The interest rate on the rest of your mortgage payments will be calculated gross.

If you pay income tax at a rate higher than the standard one then you can still benefit from mortgage interest relief at source. However, do remember to inform your tax office so they can give you the extra tax relief to which you are entitled through your tax coding.

Another major tax benefit is that your house is exempt from capital gains tax. This means that so long as the house is your principal private residence you will pay no tax on any profits you make when you sell. For most people, profits from their home is the main way they manage to build up a nestegg.

Interest rates

Building societies used to charge a standard mortgage rate which was recommended by the Building Societies Association. However, as a result of increased competition building societies now set their own rates, as banks and specialist mortgage lenders. Obviously, these will tend to be more in line with the various competitors, but at times there can be a significant difference in rates charged by the various lenders.

They are also quoted in the form of APRs, or Annual Percentage Rates. This should help customers compare rates on a fair basis. The annual percentage includes any charges such as arrangement fees as well as the interest rate itself. In fact the simplest and most effective means of comparison is to check the different sums you would be asked to pay each month.

Building societies still tend to quote the basic or nominal rate of interest but they will also quote the APR, if requested to do so, so that you can compare it directly with other lenders.

Rates are rather like the proverbial grand old Duke of York, they go up and down. Keep an eye out for changes in interest rates. These are reported in the national papers. However, your repayments may not change straight away. Some lenders have a policy of only adjusting repayments once a year. This irons out short term fluctuations in the interest rate and saves too many costly changes. If rates go up some lenders will give you the choice of either increasing your repayment or keeping the repayments at the same level and simply extending the mortgage term.

If your mortgage has a long time to run, then this is often the best option. Rates may come down again in a few months' time, allowing your mortgage term to be reduced again. There seems little point in worrying about extending your mortgage from, say, twenty-two years to twenty-three years. Those of you with an endowment mortgage just have to grin and bear it. If you have a fixed rate mortgage, you will not need to worry about any changes in the size of your monthly repayments.

Additional costs

While the most important consideration when you are buying a property is whether or not you can afford to repay the mortgage, don't forget that there are other bills to pay en route to your new front door. Try to cost everything out from the beginning so you do not find yourself with any nasty unanticipated bills.

1. Mortgage arrangement fee

Many mortgage lenders, notably the banks, charge a flat fee for simply arranging the mortgage. Arrangement fees vary, but they can be £50 to £100 depending on the lender. Always ask in advance whether such a fee will be charged and try negotiating a lower charge if you can.

2. Valuation fee

Before a bank or building society will give you a mortgage, it will want a valuation and inspection of the property. You pay for this. The fees vary. As a rough rule of thumb allow around £95 for a £50,000 house.

3. Surveyor's fee

You may want a survey of your own carried out on the property. As a half-way measure you can ask for a House Buyer's Report to be carried out, which, although it will cost you rather more than the straight valuation report, will at least give you a better idea of the state of the house. Once again costs vary, but on a £50,000 house you would be charged around £200. Alternatively, you may decide to go the whole hog and opt for a full structural survey. This is a much fuller inspection and will cost £275 to £600 for the average three bedroom house.

4. Solicitors' fees

Unless you are doing your own conveyancing, you will have to pay a solicitor to do the work for you. If you do not already have a solicitor you can either get one recommended by friends or family, or ask your local Citizens' Advice Bureau. Better still use the same solicitor as the company arranging your mortgage, as this will reduce your bill. Some firms of solicitors now advertise their conveyancing services in the local papers.

Ask your solicitors for an estimate before they start work. If they can't give you a quote, ask them why not. Do not merely go for the cheapest firm, try to take into account their local reputation. In general solicitors' fees will cost between 0.59% and 1% plus VAT of the property value.

5. Lender's solicitors' fees

The bank or building society arranging the mortgage will use their own solicitor to process the mortgage application. Their fees will be based on the size of the loan. Fees will vary depending on the size of the mortgage. You can halve your solicitors' bill by opting to use the same solicitor as the firm arranging your mortgage.

6. Land registry fees

If the property you are buying is registered with the land registry for the first time, you pay a fee according to the price of the property. However, if the house has already been registered, the fees for changing the name of the registered owner are not based on the price of the property but decided on an ad hoc basic.

HOW THE LAND REGISTRY FEES ADD UP:

House Price	First Registration
£20,000	£30
£30,000	£40
£40,000	£55
£50,000	£75
£100,000	£450

7. Stamp duty

If the price paid for the house is over £30,000 then stamp duty is payable at the rate of 1% of the total price of the house. If the purchase price includes money for fixtures and fittings, you should deduct the cost of these from the house price. Stamp duty is levied only on the purchase price of the house itself. It is automatically added to your bill and the seller's solicitor will pass the money direct to the Inland Revenue.

8. Removal costs

These vary dramatically. Allow up to £300 for moving the contents of a three bedroom house.

9. Buildings insurance

Most lenders will insist you insure your property. Unlike home contents insurance where costs vary dramatically, most buildings insurance policies cost similar amounts. You should allow roughly £115 on a £50,000 house.

HOW THE COSTS MOUNT UP*

	£
Valuation fee	95.00
Surveyor's fee (structural survey)	300.00
Solicitor's fee	250.00
Lender's solicitor's fee	72.50
Land registry fee	55.00
Stamp duty	400.00
Removal costs	200.00
Buildings insurance	80.00
Total cost †	£1,452.50

*The additional out-of-pocket expenses involved in purchasing a registered property worth £40,000 with a £25,000 mortgage.

†If you obtain your mortgage through a broker you may be charged an additional arrangement fee of £50.00.

CHAPTER THREE: COUNTDOWN TO PURCHASE

The long hard slog of house hunting is over. You've found the home of your dreams – or at least one you feel you can live in at the price you can afford. It's an exciting time and you'll feel like moving in as soon as you can. But you'll have to be patient and hold your horses for the next few weeks while the most important part of the homebuying process unfolds.

It could take six to eight weeks from start to finish for all sorts of reasons. Firstly, the legal formalities themselves have to be completed, but you could also be held up by things beyond your or your solicitor's control. Say, for instance, you are buying from Mr and Mrs A, who in turn are buying from Mr B, who is buying from Miss C. If Mr B backs out of the deal because he doesn't like the survey report of Miss C's property, she will have to look for another buyer and Mr B for another property. Mr and Mrs A will have to wait while Mr B continues his search and are highly unlikely to move into temporary accommodation just so you can move in. A break in the chain can hold everyone up.

First steps

Organising the mortgage and survey If you're sensible you will have already asked several potential lenders what you can borrow, and probably sorted out what type of mortgage you want. Some building societies give prospective borrowers a written indication of the amount they can borrow, subject to a satisfactory valuation of the property. It is usually valid for three months provided your circumstances don't change. Now's the time to go back to the building society or bank you have chosen and apply formally for your mortgage by filling in an application form.

Forget about any possible problems ahead for the moment and, as soon as you've found a home you like, make the owner an offer 'subject to contract'. At this stage you are not committed to anything. Nor, incidentally, are they. So just as you can bargain over the price later, if you discover there's something wrong with the property, for example, so they can sell to another buyer who offers them more money.

In Scotland the position is different. There an offer is legally binding and will be made by your solicitor once you have your mortgage and valuation.

What should you offer?

It's important to find out just where you should pitch your offer to avoid paying more than you need or losing a property you've set your heart on because your offer is too low. In Sheffield, for instance, the custom is for sellers to ask for offers around a certain price and for potential buyers to offer more than the asking price. This is quite different from many other towns where it's usual to offer less than the asking price. In this case the seller often, after discussion with his estate agent, may pitch the price higher than he really believes he can get in the expectation that it will be argued down by the buyer.

Make sure you know the system in the area you want to buy – perhaps by asking your local building society manager or solicitor. This is particularly important if you're moving to a new area and don't know the offer rules. Watch out if the price is just above £30,000. If you pay more than £30,000 for the house you'll have to pay stamp duty at 1% on the whole price – that's £305 on a house costing £30,500, for example. Better instead to offer £30,000 for the house and pay £500 separately for the carpets and curtains.

If you are really keen on the property and want the owners to know that you are seriously interested in buying there is no harm in making a verbal offer – you cannot be held to this if you later decide, for whatever reason, to change your mind. Say that the offer is 'subject to contract and survey', and include these words if you make a written offer. This means you can get out of the deal if you discover that the property is not worth the price you've offered or you find another property you'd rather buy.

It's difficult not to get excited about buying a new home, but try to keep a clear head and not to set your heart on one particular property. 'There's many a slip twixt cup and lip' goes the old saying and nowhere is that more true than in the homebuying process. Even after you have made your mind up that you want the house and an offer has been made you can still be 'gazumped' if someone else comes along with a higher offer.

Gazumping takes place when house prices are booming and there is a great demand for properties. It may seem morally reprehensible to you, but sellers looking for the best price for their property would be foolish to turn away a buyer offering a higher price, even if they've already agreed in principle to sell at a lower one. This cannot happen in Scotland where once an offer has been accepted it is legally binding.

So the sooner you get the legal process moving towards 'exchange of contracts' the better. Once this exchange has taken place both you and the seller are legally committed to the deal. Try to avoid getting involved in a 'contract race'. This can happen if a seller agrees to sell to more than one buyer, saying the first to exchange contracts gets the property.

Sellers sometimes employ tactics like this to speed up a sale, but only one prospective buyer will be lucky while the others suffer unnecessary expense and heartache in the process. Contract races may also backfire on the seller because solicitors usually advise their homebuying clients not to get involved, so the seller may end up with no buyers at all.

You'll know if someone else is seriously interested in the same property as you because the seller's solicitor must notify your solicitor if more than one contract for the same property has been sent out to prospective buyers. Decide then, with the advice of your solicitor, if you want to go ahead or look for another property.

If you don't already know it get the seller's full name, address and telephone number and ask for the same details about his solicitor. Pass on details of your own solicitor, if you already have one.

Go back to your building society or bank and ask them to confirm your loan. This may take a few days. They will want to check that the facts you give in the application – your income, for example – are correct and that the property you want to buy is good enough security for the amount you hope to borrow. So it may be a few days before you get confirmation of your loan. You too will want to know that your dream home is not riddled with dry rot or about to fall down so some kind of survey is needed.

There are three main types:

Valuation report
Homebuyer's report
Full structural survey

Valuation report

This is carried out solely for the lender's benefit and as far as the building society is concerned is a legal requirement. The aim of the valuation report is for the lender to check that the property is worth at least what you are planning to borrow. If so, the lender knows it won't be out of pocket if you default on your mortgage because the property can normally be sold for as much as you borrowed to pay off the outstanding debt. This is particularly important when you are borrowing 100% of the purchase price.

It is not a detailed property survey and there could still be quite serious defects in the property which are not revealed by the inspection for the valuation report.

The table shows the charges currently levied by the Nationwide Anglia Charges do vary from lender to lender, some include VAT, some don't, and you may have to pay the valuer's travelling expenses as well. So make sure you know the costs involved before going ahead.

The fee is levied on the asking price of the property, not the price you end up paying. The report may put a lower valuation on your property than the price you're being asked to pay. This need not mean there are any serious problems – merely that the seller is trying to get the best price possible. And this gives you a chance to go back and haggle with the seller over the purchase price if you want. More seriously, the valuation report may reveal defects that need expensive repair work.

In these circumstances your bank or building society will probably scale down the amount of money it is prepared to lend you, leaving you to find more out of your own pocket. If you decide you still want to go ahead with the purchase you'll almost certainly want to negotiate a lower price with the seller.

If quite substantial repairs are needed your lender may not only scale down the loan it is prepared to offer, but hold

Applicaton Fees Report & Valuation

Purchase price £	Fee £
Up to 40,000	75
40,001 – 60,000	90
60,001 – 70,000	105
70,001 – 80,000	120
80,001 – 90,000	125
90,001 – 100,000	135
100,001 – 120,000	145
120,001 – 140,000	155
140,001 – 160,000	165
160,001 – 180,000	175
180,001 – 200,000	185
200,001 – 225,000	210
225,001 – 250,000	235
250,001 – 275,000	260
275,001 – 300,000	300
Over 300,000	By agreement

Source: Nationwide Anglia Building Society. Spring 1991

back some of the money as well until the work is completed, called a 'retention'. You will have to find the money to carry out these repairs yourself, usually with a short-term bridging loan from a bank repaid when the work is completed and the rest of the mortgage is released. Many building societies have decided to offer personal banking and loan services under new powers granted to them earlier this year and the Anglia expects to introduce unsecured loans later in 1987.

When carrying out a valuation the building society or bank valuer takes into account factors such as the location of the property, e.g. good residential district, near to shops and schools, values of houses round about, as well as its apparent state of repair, but this report is not a guarantee of a fault-free property.

Homebuyer's report and valuation

This takes a much more detailed look at the structure and general state of repair of the property you want to buy as well as providing a valuation for the building society or bank. Your lender will arrange the report to be carried out for you.

It costs roughly double what you would pay for a valuation report alone. Again the fee is based on the asking price of the property, not the price you end up paying.

Homebuyer's Report Fees

Purchase £	Application Fee £
Up to 40,000	180
40,001 – 60,000	200
60,001 – 70,000	220
70,001 – 80,000	240
80,001 – 90,000	255
90,001 – 100,000	270
101,001 – 120,000	285
120,001 – 140,000	300
140,001 – 160,000	315
160,001 – 180,000	330
180,001 – 200,000	340
200,001 – 225,000	365
225,001 – 250,000	395
250,001 – 275,000	420
275,001 – 300,000	460
Over 300,000	By agreement

The above fees incorporate the Statutory Report and Valuation Fee and The Home Buyer's Report Fee on which VAT is included.

Source: Nationwide Anglia Mortgage Approvals. Spring 1991

So when should you opt for a Homebuyer's Report and Valuation and what do you get for your money? If you're buying a brand new house or flat then you probably needn't bother if the property is covered by a National House Building Council warranty.

In fact, the Building Societies' Association has recommended that its member societies should not lend on properties less than ten years old, unless these are covered by the NHBC warranty – or an architect's certificate that gives similar protection if you are buying a one-off property. The NHBC has set standards of workmanship and the type of materials and design used by builders who are registered with it and you are protected if these standards are not met.

During the first two years of purchase the builder must put right, at his own expense, any defects resulting from his failure to comply with the NHBC's standards. If the builder has gone out of business the NHBC will arrange for another to do the work, again at the builder's expense. You must complain to the builder, in writing, within the first two years of any defects, or direct to the NHBC if your builder is no longer in business.

From the third to the tenth year onwards you may also be able to claim financial help towards the cost of putting right structural defects that are not covered elsewhere, e.g. by your buildings insurance. The maximum amount of cover on NHBC certificates being issued now is £500,000, even if your home costs more than this or the repairs turn out to be more expensive. Current certificates include cover for the cost of having to pay for rented or hotel accommodation while your home is being repaired.

There is a similar sort of scheme to cover newly converted flats and houses that lasts for six years. Not every conversion is covered – the NHBC say they turn down more properties than they agree to cover – so do make sure that your property is, by checking with the NHBC or asking your solicitor to do it.

So much for a new home, but if your home is older it makes a great deal of sense to have a Homebuyer's Report and Valuation. Although it's a popular view that older properties were built to last, it's probably more true to say that some of the construction methods used then would not be acceptable today. It's also worth bearing in mind that homes built in the Thirties are now fifty years old, or more. So even though they may have emerged unscathed from the batterings of war-time, it's not surprising that many of them need patching up now or have developed problems through lack of proper maintenance.

For these homes a closer look is needed and a relatively new type of survey, the Homebuyer's Report, is now offered by most lenders. This is based on models prepared by the Royal Institution of Chartered Surveyors, the Incorporated Society of Valuers and Auctioneers and the Royal Institute of British Architects. There is an equivalent Flat Buyer's Report.

A surveyor carrying out a Homebuyer's Report and Valuation will look carefully at all parts of the house that are readily visible or accessible, including the loft if there is a trap door. He will usually check the wiring and plumbing, as far as he can, and lift drain covers. He won't normally inspect under floors – after all, at this stage you are not committed to buying the property and it's a bit much to expect the current owners to be very happy about a surveyor, or perhaps a string of surveyors, tearing up their fitted carpets and lifting floor boards. Neither will he clamber up ladders to inspect at close quarters a roof that is more than ten feet above the ground.

The limitations of this type of survey won't normally matter. A reputable surveyor should be able to spot tell-tale signs of trouble without going over the property with a fine tooth comb – particularly the presence of damp or subsidence which cost the most to put right.

If the property is neither brand new, nor pre-war, a Homebuyer's Report still makes sense if you suspect something could be amiss. You might also ask an electrician to inspect the wiring and a builder any repairs. Many firms give free estimates for work that needs doing, or charge a small fee.

The older your property, the more sensible it is to have a Homebuyer's Report and Valuation. And if the home you want to buy was built pre-1919 then a full structural survey normally makes sense.

Full structural survey

The fees for this type of survey vary according to the size and age of the property and the scope of the inspection. Although the lender can put you in touch with the right surveyor for the job it is up to you to agree the price.

As a guide the fee for a three bedroom house could range from £275 - £600 with travel expenses and VAT payable on top. You may also find yourself paying extra for tests by specialists if these are recommended by your surveyor. The survey might take half a day to a day. Although this type of survey does not usually include a valuation for the building society you can usually arrange for this to be carried out at the same time, possibly saving yourself some money.

You'd have to be pretty serious about a property to spend this sort of money, but in return you get a comprehensive and technical survey saying exactly what needs to be done – and this could provide you with a useful bargaining tool. You are perfectly entitled to ask for a reduction in the purchase price to cover the cost of putting any problems right. The survey will also give you a useful guide to the maintenance you can expect to have to do on the property in the future.

Making it legal

You can do most of the legal work connected with a house purchase yourself – if you have plenty of time and are not put off by the legal jargon you'll come across. However, if you're buying your home with a mortgage, your building society or bank will insist that a solicitor carries out the legal work on the loan, which you have to pay for. The cost of this works out much cheaper if the same solicitor is also acting for you on your house move.

If you're thinking of 'doing it yourself' be warned – buying and selling homes brings out the worst in people, so rather than get bogged down in arguments appoint a solicitor to do the hard work for you. Solicitors who specialise in conveyancing – that is, the process of transferring the ownership of a property from one person to another – deal with hundreds of house moves every month. They know all the tricks that potential buyers and sellers get up to and can help hurry things along if one of the cogs in the housebuying wheel begins to stall.

What it costs

There are no fixed fees now for conveyancing and you will have to contact several firms for an estimate of the costs involved. You might be pleasantly surprised if you haven't moved for a while or are buying for the first time.

Legal fees have dropped dramatically in recent years from perhaps 2% of the property's purchase or sale price to around 0.5 – 0.75% now. That's a possible legal bill of £125 – £188 if you're buying a £25,000 house against perhaps £500 just a few years ago.

Even in a fairly small area prices can vary quite dramatically. A recent survey by *Which?* magazine found that the most expensive firm in a town might still be more than three times as costly as the cheapest, so it pays to make a few phone calls. Some solicitors are still wary of giving estimates – usually because their fees are hopelessly uncompetitive, but you're quite entitled to ask for an estimate of costs. There's even a special Law Society form on which solicitors can set out their estimates called 'Domestic Conveyancing Charges'.

Cost isn't everything, of course, so ask around amongst your friends and colleagues before deciding on a solicitor or ask your building society manager to recommend two or three. There's no point choosing the cheapest firm you can find, for instance, if the service they offer is not up to scratch, and it's just as useful to hear about firms which have done a disappointing job as to hear glowing reports.

It usually makes sense to use a solicitor based in the area where you want to buy. He or she will be used to dealing with the estate agents, building society managers, insurance brokers and local authorities in the area and will know quickly how to sort out potential problems. You'll have the added benefit of being able to discuss your move face to face with your solicitor.

That said, there is nothing to stop you taking advantage of the fact that legal fees vary enormously around the country. London solicitors are likely to have much higher overheads than those practising in Yorkshire, for instance, so must charge more to make a profit. If you live in London ask friends based out of town to recommend the names of local solicitors or look for names and addresses in the Solicitors' Regional Directory at reference libraries.

You'll have to weigh the benefits of a potentially much lower conveyancing fee against the disadvantage of not being able to pop in to see your solicitor if things start to go awry. But if you're happy to discuss things over the telephone and the solicitor is satisfied he can act at a distance then you could save yourself hundreds of pounds.

Don't be surprised if your final bill looks much higher than the solicitor's estimate of his own costs. It will also include the stamp duty charge – 1% of the purchase price if this is more than £30,000 – and Land Registry charges. These range from £35 for a £25,000 house up to £150 for a £90,000 one, less if the property is being registered for the first time.

Cut-price conveyancing

A note of warning should be sounded about non-solicitor conveyancers. More and more cut-price conveyancing firms are advertising their services, but the apparent bargain basement fees quoted in the ads may not be all they seem. It is still an offence for anyone other than a solicitor or a licensed convey-ancer to charge a fee for conveyancing. The new breed of licensed conveyancers are people who obtain a conveyancing licence by passing, or being exempted from, an examination set by the Council of Licensed Conveyancers. Potential non-solicitor conveyancers will need at least ten years' experience of conveyancing before they can even take the test. So far only a transitional test has been introduced and there sre estimated to be fewer than 200 new licensed conveyancers in the country. Firms currently advertising cut-price conveyancing get round the problem of prosecution by getting a solicitor to draft the conveyance which legally transfers the ownership of the property.

Anyone can set up a conveyancing business and is free from the rules and regulations which cover solicitors and safeguard members of the public. It's not even necessary for

56

a conveyancing business to keep its own and the money of its clients in separate accounts – unlike solicitors who must, by law, keep the general business money and their client's money in separate accounts. Also, by law, solicitors must carry professional indemnity insurance to cover the cost of negligence claims against them. Cut-price conveyancing firms needn't bother. Some conveyancing firms are undoubtedly scrupulous in their dealings with the public and offer a good service, but is it worth taking the risk for the sake of saving a few pounds?

In fact, the saving may end up being rather less than you imagine. Those flat fees of, say, £99 advertised by conveyancing firms do not always tell the whole story. If you're taking out a mortgage to buy your home there will also be some legal work to carry out on behalf of the building society or bank which you have to pay for. The fees quoted by non-conveyancing firms usually do not include the fee you have to pay for this legal work whereas a solicitor's estimate normally does. This could add substantially to the cost of using a non-solicitor conveyancer and cause hold-ups in the buying process. Before going ahead with any conveyancing estimate make sure you know exactly what it covers and whether the price includes VAT.

Incidentally, if you haven't made a will and feel that you should now that you're about to take on some real financial responsibilities speak to the solicitor who's doing your conveyancing. He may well draw up a will at a special low price because he's also got your conveyancing business.

The legal process

Before you finally select your solicitor make sure the building society or bank is happy for him or her to carry out the legal work on your mortgage. You are responsible for the lender's legal fees in connection with the mortgage and can save money if one solicitor acts for both you and the lender.

Exchange of contracts

Once your mortgage application has been approved and your offer made and accepted 'subject to contract' your solicitor moves into top gear, investigating the legal profile of the ·

57

property before committing you to a purchase. Before starting on this work he or she will write to the sellers, or their solicitor, confirming the offer you have made 'subject to contract'.

Then he'll start the legal process by sending off a 'local search' to the local authority responsible for the area in which your home is situated. This consists of a number of questions about the property. Among the most important are:

● Are the roads serving the property maintained at the expense of the local authority? – if not the cost will have to be met by the residents.

● Are there any road proposals nearby which may affect the property? – you don't want to find yourself living next to a motorway within the next few years.

● Is the property in a conservation area, a smoke control zone or a clearance area? – if so you might find yourself bound by restrictions you could find onerous or expensive, e.g. building an extension in a certain type of stone, or losing your home under a compulsory purchase order.

A local search normally costs around £15, which you have to pay for whether the purchase finally goes through or not. You may also have to pay for special searches, e.g. to British Coal if your home is built over or near an old coal mine. Searches are sent off as soon as you instruct your solicitor to start the legal ball rolling, but it can take local authorities two to six weeks or even more to reply to the questions – so, be patient!

Meanwhile the seller's solicitor will be preparing the contract. This sets out the terms of agreement between you and the seller and includes, among other things, a full description of the property, often including a plan, the price and any restrictions affecting your use of the property. This contract is then checked by your own solicitor to make sure everything is in order. It may need to be changed, for example, if you or your solicitor on your behalf has negotiated a lower price following a survey. You may be asked to sign the contract at this stage. Don't worry. You are still not legally committed to go ahead, but having the contract already signed means that the exchange of contracts can take place quickly once the initial legal formalities have been concluded.

As well as asking the local authority questions your solicitor will also be quizzing the sellers and their solicitors. Amongst other things your solicitor will want to know:

● Whether there are any disputes affecting the property, e.g. arguments over where the boundary lies.

● What 'extras' are included in the sale, e.g. whether you are getting a kitchen full of equipment or whether the sellers are taking everything, down to the last light bulb, with them.

● Whether you will get the benefit of any guarantees relating to the property e.g. damp proofing guarantee.

● Whether the seller knows of any physical defects affecting the property, but of course you should make sure of the property's condition yourself with a survey.

Once these formalities have been completed your solicitor is ready to exchange the contract you have signed with the one signed by the sellers. At this stage you will need to pay a deposit. Traditionally this was 10% of the purchase price, but these days might be far less. Even if you are getting a 100% mortgage you will have to find the money for the deposit yourself – you cannot get part of your mortgage at this stage. So it's worth finding out in advance from your solicitor what deposit is likely to be necessary so that you can arrange for the money to be available, e.g. from your savings, a bank or building society loan.

If you're selling one house and buying another you will be able to use the deposit received from your purchaser towards your own deposit on exchange of contracts. When you exchange contracts both you and the seller are legally committed to going ahead with the sale. The deposit you pay is not returnable if you fail to complete the deal and you could be asked to pay the whole of the purchase price.

It's important that buildings insurance to cover the new property is taken out in your name at this stage because, from now on, you are legally responsible for it. This is normally arranged by the lender if you are buying with a mortgage, but if you're paying cash make sure buildings insurance arrangements are made. Your solicitor should be able to advise you.

Never exchange contracts until you are sure you have the money to pay for the property, i.e. that you have a firm offer of a mortgage from a building society or bank. When contracts are exchanged a date is usually agreed when you can finally move into your new home – the completion date.

Completion

Completion usually takes place two to four weeks after contracts have been exchanged. The gap is necessary for two reasons. Firstly, it gives you and the seller time to make removal arrangements, to arrange final readings of the gas and electricity meters, and to notify the rating departments and water authority. Secondly, it enables your solicitor to finalise the legal work. This includes making sure the seller has the right to sell the property and to prepare the conveyance – the document that transfers ownership of property from the seller to you.

Your solicitor will also arrange for your purchase money – usually a mortgage from a building society or bank – to be ready for the day of completion. This will go direct to your solicitor and then be passed on to the seller's solicitor. You don't have to worry about collecting the money yourself. It's usually up to you to arrange when and where you collect the keys from the seller. If you're buying a brand new house, or a vacant property, you may be offered the keys on exchange of contracts, but only to measure up for carpets or to tidy up, not to move in.

After completion – when, hopefully, you are happily ensconced in your new home – your title deeds will be sent to your building society or bank and remain there for the lifetime of your mortgage as security for the loan. If you're not using a mortgage to buy your home you can keep the deeds yourself, but it's safer to lodge them with your solicitor or in a deed box at the bank in case of fire or burglary.

It's been a long, probably worrying and certainly expensive time, but try and keep back a few pounds of your hard-earned savings and crack open a bottle of champagne on completion day. It's the best way of setting yourself up for the final part of the housebuying process – the big move in.

Countdown to purchase

10 Apply to your building society or bank for a Mortgage Pledge certificate. Make an offer, subject to contract and survey.

9 Apply formally for your mortgage.

8 Ask your solicitor to put the legal process in motion.

7 Decide what type of survey you want. Arrange with lender. Pay appropriate fee.

6 Ask electrician/plumber/timber specialist to look at the property and give estimates for necessary work.

5 Re-negotiate on price if seller is asking more than property is worth.

4 Exchange contracts. Make sure you have the deposit ready. Arrange buildings insurance. Agree completion date.

3 Get estimates from removal firms. Provisionally book them for completion date, confirm nearer the time.

2 Arrange final readings of gas and electricity meters. Inform rating department of change of ownership. Arrange reconnection dates for electricity, gas, telephone. Ask if you can measure up for curtains, carpets, etc.

1 Completion day – and lift off! Collect the keys – they're all yours.

Buying a home in Scotland

The legal process involved in buying a home in Scotland starts much earlier than in England and Wales because, once your offer is accepted, it becomes a binding contract which neither the buyer nor seller can escape from. This is different from England where you make your offer 'subject to contract' and both you and the seller can withdraw without penalty if, for example, a survey reveals problems with the property or another buyer comes along and offers a higher price. There are two main areas of the Scottish legal aspects of homebuying – the bargain and conveyancing.

The bargain

In Scotland, the contract for the purchase of a home invariably takes the form of a written offer to buy and a written acceptance, usually set out in letters. Because of this the contract is referred to as 'missives'. Once the offer has been made and accepted it takes the form of a completed and binding bargain that obliges the buyer to buy and the seller to sell.

It is vital, therefore, that you are sure of the condition of the property being purchased and you know for certain that you can finance the purchase before an offer is made. Buyers in Scotland, or their solicitors, must notify the building society that they would like to make an offer before going beyond the 'missive', the point of no return.

The offer to purchase is prepared by the buyer's solicitor who signs it on the buyer's behalf. In most cases, a seller invites offers for his or her property over a certain price. This is called the 'asking' or 'upset' price. It is an indication of what the seller hopes to get for his property, but as the Scottish system is effectively one of blind bidding the buyer has to decide, with the help of his or her solicitor, what price to offer in order to be successful.

The seller may set a closing date by which offers have to be submitted. There is only a chance to negotiate on price when noone else is interested in buying the property. The buyer's offer may also contain a time limit, by which the seller must accept or decline. If a property is advertised at a 'fixed price' this means the seller intends to accept the first offer of that amount received.

The conveyancing

Once the offer has been accepted and the bargain made the solicitor begins the process of transferring ownership of the property. He or she obtains title deeds of the property from the seller's solicitor and makes sure there are no defects. The solicitor will also advise on 'burdens and servitudes', rather like restrictive covenants in England, which might restrict use of the property. Together with the seller's solicitor he or she also prepares a 'draft of the disposition' – the deed transferring title to the property – and prepares the loan documents.

When the legal work has been completed the buyer pays the agreed price to the seller in exchange for a properly signed 'disposition' transferring the house from seller to buyer. This is called the 'date of entry' when the buyer can take possession of the property. There is no hard and fast rule but, on average, the date of entry is usually four to six weeks after the contract to purchase has been completed.

While most houses in Scotland are freehold, as in England, most flats are 'feudal' – more like freehold than the leasehold form of tenure that is common for English flats. The title deeds usually set out each individual flat owner's responsibilities for maintaining the common parts of the block. If not these are covered by the Law of the Tenement. In both cases the responsibilities can be enforced legally.

Useful addresses

Building Societies Association
3 Savile Row
London W1X 1AF
Telephone: 071-437 0655

Free leaflets on aspects of housebuying

Law Society
113 Chancery Lane
London WC2A 1PL
Telephone: 071-242 1222

Free leaflet 'Why you should use a solicitor'

National House Building Council
58 Portman Place
London W1N 4BU
Telephone: 071-637 1248

Free leaflets on the NHBC warranty scheme

Royal Institution of Chartered Surveyors
12 Great George Street
Parliament Square
London SW1P 3AD
Telephone: 071-222 7000

Free leaflets include 'Mortgage valuations explained', 'Buying your home', 'What is a structural survey' and 'Flat and Housebuyer's Report Explained'.

CHAPTER FOUR:
INSURING YOUR INTERESTS

All householders need insurance. You should not dismiss this as an unnecessary additional expense that can be reduced if the budget is tight. Disaster may be lurking just around the corner, so it is vital to obtain the right insurance cover. Your insurance requirements fall into three basic categories. You need to insure the loan, your home and its contents.

Why insure?

According to the estimates roughly 25% of all householders in this country do not have any insurance cover for their possessions and a much higher proportion are seriously underinsured. Put simply, this means that probably as many as half the people in your street would be out of pocket if they had a fire or a burglary. And out of pocket can mean they stand to lose several thousand pounds in many cases.

Insurance is too important to be left to the last minute. Grabbing the cheapest option available may seem fine in the short-term, but could lose you pounds later on. You've sunk all your savings into your new home, committed yourself to a mortgage that is likely to swallow up all your spare cash for the next few years, spent hundreds of pounds on furnishing and equipping your new home. Proper insurance can protect this huge personal investment against life's disasters – great and small. It is worth spending time working out your insurance requirements and looking for the best deal.

Let's start by looking at insurance for your home itself. You can either insure it separately or opt for one of the comparatively new type of combined insurance policies which cover both your property and its contents. Whatever option you pick the aim is to buy the correct amount of insurance at the most reasonable price. This will depend on three basic factors: the type of property, its location and the value of your home and possessions.

Buildings insurance

The institution lending you the money to buy your home will insist that you take out a buildings insurance policy. This is as much in their interests as yours. It means that there will always be enough money to repair or re-build the house if it is damaged or destroyed. The house is, after all, the institution's main security for lending you so much money.

In order to comply with current Office of Fair Trading recommendations the building society or bank has to give you the chance to choose a policy from a list of at least three insurance companies. In practice, you will find the policies tend to be very similar in terms of cover and cost. If you'd prefer an insurance company that is not on the list, ask the building society or bank if you can use an alternative of your own choice. They are not obliged to accept your choice, although most do nowadays, especially if your property has any unusual features such as a thatched roof which may not be covered by the standard type of policy from a company on their own list. Most building societies make a charge of between £15 and £35 to cover the increased administrative costs in which they are involved when you arrange your own cover.

What, you may wonder, is 'buildings insurance'? A buildings insurance policy will cover the structure of your house – the foundation, walls, floors, doors, windows, roof, plumbing, fixed electrical wiring, decorations and insulation. It should also include the various permanent fixtures and fittings that are immovable and which would be left behind when you come to sell the property. The only exceptions to this are fitted carpets and television aerials, which are regarded as contents items. A buildings insurance policy will also cover garages, greenhouses, sheds, paths, patios, walls, fences and gates.

The policy will pay the cost of repairs or re-building if your home is damaged by fire, storms, floods, subsidence, riot or malicious damage, impact by aircraft, vehicles or falling trees or water escaping from the plumbing or a washing machine. If you live in an area that is known to be prone to subsidence or flooding, you may find damage by these causes may be excluded from the policy or only be available for an additional payment.

Most policies pay the full cost of replacement or repairs, provided the house has been properly maintained and insured to its full value. Some insurance policies will, however, make a deduction for wear and tear. This means that if the house is in a better condition after the repairs are completed than before the mishap struck, you will have to pay the cost of this improvement. These policies are not so common now.

Whichever type of policy you choose you may have to pay the first £15 to £50 of any claim, the so-called 'excess' in insurance jargon. This may rise to £500 if you have to make a claim for subsidence or similar damage caused by earth movements. Accidental damage to glass, sanitary fittings, underground water, oil, gas, sewage and drain pipes should be included. For example, if you put a spade through the electricity cable that serves your home, you can claim against your buildings policy. Other costs that are usually covered include architect's and surveyor's fees, but not those incurred in preparing a claim, the cost of temporary accommodation (up to 10% of the total value of the policy) and your public liability to other people.

This last section will give you cover for between £500,000 and £1 million if you, or a member of your family, has to pay damages to someone who is injured or who has their property damaged as a result of your negligence. For example, if a slate falls from your roof, which has not been properly maintained, and injures a pedestrian or damages a car. Accidents of this sort are all too common with older houses in inner city areas.

There is a second type of buildings insurance available offering greater protection, including accidental damage cover. For instance, if you put your foot through the ceiling whilst in the loft then you can claim. This extra cover is more expensive.

One restriction which you'll find in all types of buildings insurance policies is a clause severely limiting the cover if you go away for more than a stated period, usually sixty days. In most cases, the insurance company will cut out the cover for damage caused by escaping water, by thieves trying to enter your home, malicious actions (vandalism) and accidental damage.

You buy cover under a buildings insurance policy on the basis of the sum you would need to re-build your home. A cheap policy, with several restrictions, might cost as little as £1.50 per £1,000 worth of cover. A more sophisticated policy, including additional accidental damage cover, could cost more than 30% extra at £2.10 per £1,000. You must buy sufficient buildings insurance to match the full cost of re-building your house from scratch. The amount of insurance you need has nothing to do with the market value of the property. Sometimes it will cost more to re-build a house than its market price, sometimes less.

Doing the sums

How, then, can you work out how much buildings insurance you need? Normally, the building society surveyor will suggest a figure for insurance and you will have to buy this amount of cover before the society will agree to the mortgage. The cost of re-building your house will depend upon where you live. The price of labour and materials varies from area to area. You may also find that if your particular location is known to be subject to subsidence or flood, you will be charged extra or at worst, you won't be able to buy cover for these risks at all. Table 1 gives a guide to the cost of re-building different types of property in different parts of the country based on costings in September 1986. Rebuilding costs have risen by just under 10% between autumn 1986 and spring 1988 so you should keep this in mind when reading the table. Prices vary not only by region, but also according to the type and age of your property.

REGIONS

1. London Boroughs
2. South East and North West England
   (Bedfordshire, Berkshire, Buckinghamshire, Essex, Hampshire, Hertfordshire, Kent, Oxfordshire, Surrey, East Sussex, West Sussex, Cheshire, Greater Manchester, Lancashire and Merseyside)
3. Scotland, Wales and Northern England
   (The whole of Scotland and Wales and Cleveland, Cumbria, Durham, Northumberland, Tyne & Wear)
4. East Anglia, East Midlands, West Midlands, South West, Yorkshire & Humberside and Northern Ireland
   (All other counties)

NOTES TO TABLE ONE

1. This chart has been prepared by the Building Cost Information Service of the Royal Institution of Chartered Surveyors and the majority of householders have been catered for by providing rebuilding cost information on five different house types, with average quality finish, depending on their age, size and location. Of course, it is impossible to cover all circumstances and, for

How much would it cost to re-build your home? September 1986 costings – £ per square foot (external)

		PRE 1920			1920 – 1945			1946 – DATE		
		LARGE	MEDIUM	SMALL	LARGE	MEDIUM	SMALL	LARGE	MEDIUM	SMALL
DETACHED HOUSE	Region 1	53.00	57.00	56.00	50.50	52.50	53.00	43.00	45.50	46.00
	2	46.50	50.00	49.00	44.50	46.00	46.50	37.50	40.00	40.00
	3	44.00	47.50	46.50	42.00	44.00	44.00	36.00	38.00	38.00
	4	41.50	45.00	44.00	40.00	41.50	41.50	34.00	36.00	36.00
	Typical Area ft²	3450	1700	1300	2550	1350	1050	1650	1350	1050
SEMI-DETACHED HOUSE	Region 1	51.50	52.50	52.50	54.50	52.50	52.50	39.00	41.50	44.50
	2	45.50	46.00	46.00	48.00	46.00	46.00	34.50	36.50	39.00
	3	43.00	44.00	43.50	45.50	44.00	44.00	32.50	34.50	37.00
	4	41.00	41.50	41.50	43.00	41.50	41.50	31.00	33.00	35.00
	Typical Area ft²	2300	1650	1200	1350	1150	900	1650	1350	1050
DETACHED BUNGALOW	Region 1				54.50	50.50	52.00	47.00	47.00	49.00
	2				48.00	44.50	45.50	41.00	41.50	43.00
	3	The chart does not cover			45.50	42.00	43.00	39.00	39.50	41.00
	4	pre-1920 bungalows, as few			43.00	40.00	41.00	37.00	37.00	38.50
	Typical Area ft²	such properties were built.			1650	1400	1000	1650	1350	1050
SEMI-DETACHED BUNGALOW	Region 1				56.50	57.00	50.50	45.50	46.00	47.50
	2				49.50	50.00	44.50	40.00	40.00	42.00
	3				47.00	47.50	42.00	38.00	38.00	39.50
	4				44.50	45.00	40.00	36.00	36.00	37.50
	Typical Area ft²				1350	1200	800	1350	1200	800
TERRACED HOUSE	Region 1	56.00	55.00	54.50	54.50	54.50	54.00	39.50	42.50	47.00
	2	49.00	48.00	48.00	48.00	47.50	47.00	34.50	37.50	41.50
	3	46.50	45.50	45.50	45.50	45.00	45.00	33.00	35.50	39.50
	4	44.00	43.50	43.00	43.00	43.00	42.50	31.00	33.50	37.00
	Typical Area ft²	1650	1350	1050	1350	1050	850	1650	1300	900

TABLE 1 **REBUILDING COSTS**

instance, the chart is unsuitable for certain types of property including the following:

(a) Properties which are not built mainly of brick.

(b) Properties with more than two storeys (for three-storey houses, see 'Making your own estimate') or with basements and cellars.

(c) Flats, because there are wide differences in construction and responsibilities for shared parts.

(d) Houses with special design features or of greater sizes than those described in the chart.

2. **All the figures in the chart are based on houses of average quality finish and might need adjusting.** For example, if your house is of higher quality, with luxury kitchen and sanitary fittings, floor and wall finishes and double glazing, your final figure would need to be increased by up to 25%.

3. The figures in the chart are based on rebuilding your home to its existing standard using current materials and techniques available. If older houses are required to be reinstated in exactly their original style, a professional valuation is essential.

4. All the figures in the chart include allowances for full central heating (at an approximate cost of £2,200) and demolition costs and professional fees.

To use the table you have to work out the total floor area of your home – upstairs and downstairs. If it is a three storey house only three-quarters of the floor area of the top floor should be counted. You will also have to add a figure for the cost of rebuilding your garage, if appropriate. A single pre-fabricated garage could add £2,100 and a brick built double could add as much as £6,600 to your total. The table cannot be used for a house of four or more storeys, buildings with basements or cellars, houses of unusual construction, houses with thatched roofs or buildings more than about one hundred and fifty years old. If you own a property that falls into any of these categories you should call in a valuer to give you an accurate figure for re-building. Table 2 will help you with the calculations.

Once you have an accurate figure, whether from the building society, the table or an independent valuation, you will have to work out how much your insurance will cost. Premiums are usually paid annually but payments by monthly instalments are available. Cover will be linked to a recognised index, usually the House Rebuilding Cost Index compiled by

TABLE 2   MAKING YOUR OWN ESTIMATE

Total external
area (upstairs
and down) –   sq. ft. **A**

'Per-square-foot'
rebuilding cost – £   **B**

Multiply A×B – £   **C**

Add for garage
(see below) – £   **D**

Estimate the cost of rebuilding any outbuildings, walls and
fences and any other items covered and put this figure
against E.

£   **E**

Now add C, D and E
together – £

If your policy is not index-
linked add on a suitable
allowance for inflation   £

TOTAL – £

This figure is the approximate amount for which an
average quality home should be insured (see Note 2).

GARAGES

For garages (other than integral) total rebuilding costs range
from £2,100 for a single pre-fabricated to £6,600 for a double
detached in brick. Using these as a guide, insert an appropriate
figure against D above.

Source: Building Cost Information Service of the Royal Institution
of Chartered Surveyors.

the Building Cost Information Service of the Royal Institute
of Chartered Surveyors. If you have made any major
alterations such as installing central heating, new windows
or building an extension, you should notify the insurance
company as this will alter the re-building cost for your house.
You will need to increase your policy to take account of the
alteration.

TABLE 3   INSURING YOUR PROPERTY

PROPERTY	ESTIMATED VALUE	ANNUAL PREMIUMS ON	
		BASIC POLICY	ACCIDENTAL DAMAGE INCLUDED
Medium size London semi built in 1918	£96,670	£193.40	£222.41
Small terrace house in Manchester circa 1900	£20,820	£41.60	£47.84
Large detached London house built in 1950	£139,940	£279.80	£321.77
Small semi in Edinburgh with garage, built in 1930	£43,670	£87.4	£100.51

Notes: **Basic policy worked out on rate of £2.00 per £ thousand. Accidental Damage and Cover worked out on rate of £2.30 per £ thousand.**
Source: Nationwide Anglia Mortgage Approvals. January 1991

Table 3 gives a few comparative examples of the costs of providing various levels of cover for four different types of property, based on prices and insurance charges in January 1991. Among the most difficult types of property to insure are thatched properties. Many insurance companies will give anyone with a charming thatched cottage in some rural beauty spot the thumbs down straight away. Others will push the rates up through all that picturesque thatch or refuse to insure the house against damage or fire which starts on the roof. There are a handful of insurance organisations who specialise in insurance cover for thatched properties but you could still end up paying perhaps more than double the rate of premium charged for more conventional construction homes.

There can also be specialist problems with flats. In January 1985 there was a gas explosion in a block of Putney flats in central London and one of the couples was made homeless because the insurance companies could not agree who should pay what towards the re-building costs. As a flat owner you should insist on seeing the insurance policy covering the whole block. Check this carefully, if necessary seeking advice from your building society, insurance broker or solicitor. As the law stands at the moment, a landlord or head leaseholder can buy the very minimal insurance cover on a block of flats, often only covering it against fire, leaving out vital areas such as water drainage and subsidence. If you find yourself moving into a block of flats with only this level of cover you should try hard to persuade the landlord to improve the policy.

Failing this, you can buy your own policy to fill some of the gaps in the landlord's buildings insurance policy. This additional insurance will pay towards the cost of alternative accommodation if your flat is damaged and you cannot live in it or if you cannot get access to it because of damage to other parts of the block. It will also protect you if your flat is damaged by subsidence or water. These policies will pay you the flat's market value if it remains uninhabitable for a long time. You can usually choose the time period which has to elapse before the policy pays out. The longer you wait the cheaper the policy. However, if you opt for the three year wait you may only get what your flat was worth at the time of the accident, not at the date you receive the cash. The way property prices have been moving in the last fifteen years this may prove to be an illusory saving. You should ask your financial adviser to recommend a suitable plan or put you in touch with someone who specialises in the field of home insurance. Take a copy of the landlords policy with you and try to work out in advance the extra cover you require.

Contents insurance

A contents insurance policy covers your possessions. Unlike buildings insurance policies, noone is going to insist that you insure your belongings. With the current boom in burglaries, not to insure your possessions would be foolish.

Thousands of people have fallen victim to burglary in recent years. Nobody finds it easy to cope with the trauma of a robbery but at least those with adequate insurance have the comfort of knowing they will be able to replace everything they have lost, even if the mental damage takes longer to heal.

There is plenty of choice when it comes to insuring your contents. As a result there is a much wider range of charges and it can be difficult to decide exactly which policy will suit you best. The term 'contents' actually includes everything you have in your home and any outbuildings, such as a garage (but not your car) that is not a so-called permanent fixture. The contents cover also includes fitted carpets even though they may be a more or less permanent feature. A contents insurance policy will divide your possessions up into different categories and you will find different conditions attached to each grouping. The details will be in the policy literature from the insurance company. Do read this carefully and make sure you understand it. If it is in tiny print and legal language you don't understand, go elsewhere. Many companies produce documents in what is called 'plain English' and your building society should be able to help.

Your contents policy will cover you for loss of or damage to your possessions as a result of the same causes listed in the earlier section on buildings insurance with the major addition of theft. Buildings insurance will include theft of gates, doors etc., or damage as a result of breaking and entering.

Again, you can buy a more expensive policy which includes accidental damage cover. When it comes to contents the scope for accidental damage is enormous – spilling paint on a carpet, knocking a cup of coffee over the hi-fi system, dropping a crystal lampshade to name but a few examples. People with young children should seriously consider taking out accidental damage cover with their contents policy. Although it adds to the cost, it's usually well worth the extra.

The most fundamental choice you need to make is whether to go for the cheaper indemnity cover policy or the more expensive new-for-old policy (sometimes called replacement-as-new). Indemnity cover is insurance jargon for a policy that will pay the present value of your property. This means the insurance company will make deductions for wear and tear. Generally, this type of insurance is about 20% cheaper than new-for-old cover, but it can leave you seriously out of pocket when making a claim.

The problem with indemnity cover is that when you come to replace your valuables you usually have to pay for brand new items and end up digging deep into your wallet. In the case of a five year old carpet which could have been expected to last for fifteen years, but which has been damaged by fire and claimed for, the gap between what the policy would pay and what a new carpet costs could be enormous. The insurance company would take the price of a new carpet and reduce that price by five-fifteenths, i.e. by five years out of its fifteen year estimated life. So, if the new carpet cost £120 the insurance company would pay only £80.

The main benefit of an all risks policy is that it will cover items when they are taken out of the home, even abroad. This means you don't have to buy additional insurance when you go abroad for your possessions, although you will need cancellation and medical cover. You can if you wish, add accidental damage to indemnity terms and new-for-old but there is no need to do this with an all risks policy as it automatically includes accidental damage. These three types of cover can be mixed in various ways, but the most common six types are listed below.

TABLE 4   COVERING YOUR ASSETS

TYPE OF POLICY	RANGE OF COVER
Indemnity	Pays the current value of items after a deduction for wear and tear.
Indemnity plus some new-for-old cover	This policy will give you new-for-old cover on items until they are two to three years old. It offers indemnity cover for older items.
New-for-old	Pays the current replacement value of all items, except clothes and household linen.
New-for-old with accidental damage cover	For an additional premium you can add accidental damage cover.
New-for-old with all risks (and accidental damage)	A policy that offers you the opportunity of insuring some specified items, such as cameras, on an all risks basis. You could also add some accidental damage cover to this.
All risks	Every item is covered on an all risks basis.

Indemnity cover, although better than nothing, can leave you with a hefty bill. So unless you want to do the rounds of second hand shops and jumble sales you are best avoiding indemnity cover policies. Fortunately most insurance companies have not promoted these policies too much in recent years so they are dropping out of the picture.

More common nowadays is the new-for-old policy. These policies will pay you a sufficient sum to replace any lost, damaged or stolen property at current prices. The one exception is that a deduction for wear and tear will be made for your clothes and household linen. Sometimes, when you claim, there is some difficulty in deciding what counts as an equivalent replacement, especially if the item is no longer available. Occasionally, policy holders and insurance companies cannot reach agreement and the section on claims at the end of this chapter gives a few hints on how to handle such a situation.

The other principal variation on the theme of contents cover is the all risks policy. This is a very confusing term that frequently leads to misunderstandings. 'All risks' means that the insurance policy will cover you for virtually every possible risk but it is a quite costly form of cover. Instead of giving you a long list of all the things that the policy covers, leaving you to work out what the gaps are, there is a short list of things that are not included. This usually consists of wear and tear, damage during cleaning or restoration, damage by moths, vermin or insects, and breakage of very fragile items.

The crucial question, of course, is how much is all this going to cost? Insurance companies divide the country into a number of different areas. This is done by using the postcodes and each district is given a rating based on the insurance company's experience on the level of claims. Most household claims are for theft, so the level of crime has become the most important factor in determining premiums for house contents policies in recent years. The cost of insuring your possessions if you live in an inner city is going to be relatively high, roughly twice as much as in a rural area. Inner city householders often lose out twice. They are charged more for their cover in the first place and then expected to pay a larger proportion of any claim for theft. The Prudential Assurance, for example, insist you pay the first £200 on any theft claim.

Table 5 shows some typical costs for insuring contents in different parts of the country based on charges made by insurance companies in the spring of 1988. The premiums are worked out in the same way as for buildings insurance, i.e. a rate of premium for each £1,000 of cover. Typical high risk areas would be large parts of Greater London, Manchester, Liverpool, Glasgow, Birmingham, possibly Leeds and Bristol with some companies. Medium risk areas are the remainder of our cities and the suburbs of the high risk cities. Low risk areas are rural East Anglia and the West Country. Table 5 is intended to give a flavour of the variations in costs. It is important to remember that each insurance company makes its own judgement on what it considers 'high risk' and 'low risk'. One company may put Harrow in its top rated category, others may have it in their second or third category. It is, therefore, very important to obtain at least three quotations, especially if you are a city dweller.

TABLE 5 POLICY CHARGES

TYPE OF POLICY	COST PER THOUSAND POUNDS WORTH OF COVER IN		
	HIGH RISK AREA	MEDIUM RISK AREA	LOW RISK AREA
Standard	£9.00 – £12.00	£6.00 – £7.50	£4.50 – £5.00
Cover plus	£10.50 – £13.50	£7.50 – £9.00	£6.00 – £6.50
All risks (per £100)	£2.00 – £2.50	£1.50 – £1.75	£1.00 – £1.25

Notes:
1. **Standard cover** is 'new to old', except for clothing and household linen when wear and tear will be taken into account.
2. **Cover plus** is standard cover plus accidental damage to household goods within the property.
3. **All risks** covers valuables such as jewellery, furs, precious metals etc.

Some companies offer small discounts ranging from 5% to 15% for people who install adequate security devices or belong to neighbourhood watch schemes. The number of companies offering these extra incentives is growing all the time so you should check with a building society or an insurance broker if you are interested in obtaining such a discount. However, some firms will refuse to pay a theft claim if you have not used the security devices properly at the time of the theft. Unless you believe that you could never make such a mistake you would be better off looking for another insurance company that does not impose such a condition.

After all, it is easy to forget to lock a window but a single omission of that sort and you could find your whole claim turned down by some companies.

Even if you do not opt for a policy which gives you a discount for installing security devices, you will be strongly advised by the insurance company to take proper precautions to protect your home. Some companies have booklets on security and issue policyholders with ultra-violet marker pens which can be used to identify your goods. The Association of British Insurers produces general leaflets giving hints on security which are available to the public free of charge.

If you have only a small amount of personal possessions you will have to look out for a 'minimum sum assured' on the policy. Most insurance companies have increased this in recent years to about £10,000. This is not a particularly high figure as the checklist below will show (Table 6). However, if you really do have less than that to insure you will have to shop around. A few companies offer special policies for the elderly, people in flats or furnished accommodation, and students.

Having decided what sort of policy you want the most difficult task is to work out how much cover to buy. Most people underestimate the value of their possessions. For example, £17,500 would be a fairly typical value for the contents of a three bedroom terrace house, and a large semi-detached house could quite easily have over £23,000 of contents. These estimates are based on 1991 prices.

You can use Table 6 to help your calculations. Check through your home putting in the price for each item as new. It is all too easy to overlook things and underestimate their value. For instance, if you have one hundred records it is likely to cost you at least £600 to replace them.

You should get all valuable items properly valued. This applies to works of art, antiques and jewellery. A proper valuation will save any arguments with the insurance company over the claim. As a second best the receipt and a detailed description will usually suffice for jewellery. If any one valuable item exceeds 5% of the total, then the insurance company will probably ask for a higher premium.

TABLE 6   INSURING YOUR CONTENTS
A ROOM BY ROOM GUIDE

To find the value of your home contents enter your own estimated replacement values in the space provided.

SITTING ROOM	EXAMPLE NEW PRICE	YOUR ESTIMATE
Three piece suite, chairs	£800	£
TV and Video equipment	£750	£
Hi-Fi/personal computer	£450	£
Book case (including books), tables	£300	·£
Cassettes, tapes and records	£250	£
Pictures, clocks, ornaments, lamps	£150	£
Curtains, carpets, rugs etc	£600	£
Other items		£
	Total	£

DINING ROOM	EXAMPLE NEW PRICE	YOUR ESTIMATE
Tables, chairs	£500	£
Pictures, clocks, ornaments, lamps	£100	£
Curtains, carpets, rugs etc	£400	£
China, glass and cutlery	£300	£
Sideboards, other furniture	£300	£
Other items		£
	Total	£

KITCHEN/UTILITY ROOM	EXAMPLE NEW PRICE	YOUR ESTIMATE
Washing machine, tumble dryer	£400	£
Dishwasher	£300	£
Refrigerator, freezer	£300	£
Cooker, microwave	£450	£
Table, chairs	£200	£
Crockery, cutlery, tools and utensils	£200	£
Electrical appliances	£250	£
Floor coverings, curtains	£250	£
Food, drink	£200	£
Other items		£
	Total	£

HALL, STAIRS, LANDING	**EXAMPLE NEW PRICE**	**YOUR ESTIMATE**
Furniture	£100	£
Blankets, towels and household linen	£250	£
Pictures, ornaments	£ 75	£
Curtains, carpets, rugs etc	£750	£
Other items		£
Total		£

BATHROOM	**EXAMPLE NEW PRICE**	**YOUR ESTIMATE**
Bathroom furniture, cabinet etc	£ 75	£
Floor coverings, blinds	£100	£
Other items		£
Total		£

MAIN BEDROOM	**EXAMPLE NEW PRICE**	**YOUR ESTIMATE**
Bed(s) and bedding	£300	£
Bedroom furniture	£750	£
Pictures, clocks, lamps, mirrors	£150	£
Curtains, carpets, rugs etc	£275	£
Other items		£
Total		£

OTHER BEDROOMS	**EXAMPLE NEW PRICE**	**YOUR ESTIMATE**
Bed(s) and bedding	£350	£
Bedroom furniture	£650	£
Pictures, clocks, lamps, mirrors	£150	£
Curtains, carpets, rugs etc	£300	£
Other items		£
Total		£

GARAGE/OUTBUILDINGS	**EXAMPLE NEW PRICE**	**YOUR ESTIMATE**
Garden tools	£100	£
DIY tools etc	£100	£
Lawnmower	£150	£
Garden furniture	£200	£
Other items		£
Total		£

PERSONAL EFFECTS

Clothing (excluding furs) and all other personal articles (including toys, sports equipment and pedal cycles) worn used or carried other than valuables and money.	Husband's	£
	Wife's	£
	Children	£
	Other items	£
	Total	£

VALUABLES

Jewellery, watches, articles of gold, silver and other precious metals, furs, cameras, binoculars, pictures and other works of art and collections of stamps, coins and medals.	Husband's	£
	Wife's	£
	Children	£
	Other items	£
	Total	£

| Money | Total | £ |

Now transfer all the totals to the grid below.

TOTALS	YOUR ESTIMATE
Sitting Room	£
Dining Room	£
Kitchen/Utility Room	£
Hall, Stairs, Landing	£
Bathroom	£
Main Bedroom	£
Other Bedrooms	£
Other Rooms	£
Garage/Outbuildings	£
SUB TOTAL	£
Personal effects	£
Valuables	£
Money	£
The value of your contents is ...	£

THIS IS THE SUM FOR WHICH YOU SHOULD INSURE YOUR CONTENTS

Source: Guardian Royal Exchange.

If you are thinking of taking out a policy which includes an all risks option, you should make a list of all the things that go out of the house regularly which you want insured, so you can work out a separate price for them. If you have chosen a good policy you should also find it includes options to cover pedal cycles (although expensive bikes will need a specialist policy), sports equipment, cash and credit cards (including misuse) and the contents of your deep freeze. This latter option should cover power failure, except due to strikes, contamination and theft. Again you should put all the items you want covered on these sections down on a list alongside the estimated cost of replacing them with the equivalent item at current prices.

Once you have got your totals for each part of the policy, you must insure your contents for that full amount. Never deliberately underinsure and always check each year that your total is up to date so that new items are properly covered. Some policies are index-linked but even if you have one of these you must remember to add all the items you've purchased or been given over the past twelve months.

Lastly, like a buildings insurance policy, your cover will be reduced if you leave the property unoccupied for more than sixty days a year. If you plan to go away for longer than this, contact the insurance company and find out what cover they will provide. They may increase the cover if you agree to pay extra.

Combined policies

There is a new breed of combined buildings and contents insurance policies available. These are offered mainly through building societies who are keen to obtain a larger share of the contents insurance market.

One big advantage of these policies is that they save you the time and trouble of working out the value of your possessions. What happens is that you insure your house under the buildings section in the normal way and then your contents are automatically included up to 50% of the value of the house. So, if it would cost £40,000 to re-build your house, then your contents would automatically be covered for up to £20,000.

The cost of such a policy is difficult to compare with buying insurance separately in general terms but if you are offered one of these policies you can work out which is the best deal for your particular case. In spring 1988 the premium on combined buildings and contents policies varied from £2.50 to £3.50 per £1,000 of cover in rural areas rising to as much as £5.80 per £1,000 in inner city areas. In general terms, the combined policy is good value for money if your contents are valued at or near to 50% of the rebuilding cost of your home. They tend not to be the cheapest option if your contents do not represent such a high proportion of your rebuilding costs as Table 7, which is based on estimates for inner city properties, shows.

TABLE 7   COMPARING THE COSTS OF HOME INSURANCE

	REBUILDING COST	CONTENTS VALUE	ANNUAL COST OF COMBINED POLICY	ANNUAL COST OF BUYING SEPARATE POLICIES		
				BUILDINGS	CONTENTS	BUILDINGS + CONTENTS
1.	£50,000	£17,500	£300	£100	£236.25	£336.25
2.	£60,000	£12,000	£360	£120	£162	£202
3.	£100,000	£20,000	£600	£200	£270	£470
4.	£100,000	£30,000	£600	£200	£405	£605

Assumptions
(1) Inner London rates for combined and contents policy
(2) Rates used: house and home £6.00 per £1,000; buildings only (standard) £2.00 per £1,000; and contents £13.50 per £1,000.
(3) On house and home cover, contents covered for ½ the rebuilding cost up to a maximum of £70,000, ie maximum contents cover £3,500.

How to make a claim

It is one of those unfortunate facts of life that most of us will have to make an insurance claim at some time in our lives. The secret of a successful, trouble-free claim is to gather the right information and present it to the insurance company as succinctly as possible.

You will need to know your policy number. This will be printed on your policy document which should be kept in a safe place, or your mortgage account number, if the policy was arranged through a building society. If you have lost property you will need to state the cause of the loss – theft, fire or other accident – and how it happened. If you are burgled, you should report this to the police straightaway. Your insurance company will want to know the address of the police station you contacted and the time you reported the theft. The insurance company will also need to know in the case of a damage claim whether the damage was caused by someone not normally resident with you. If so, they will want their address.

You should also tell the insurance company whether the items lost or damaged were insured under another insurance policy as well. This could happen if you have, say, a camera insured on the all risks section of your household insurance policy but also insure it on a travel insurance policy and then have it stolen when you are abroad. By telling the insurance company that it is insured under two policies you will avoid any time-consuming correspondence with the insurance company, who will be quick to investigate if they think there is any chance that you might have insured an item twice.

You will, of course, have to provide a detailed list of all items you wish to claim for as well as any estimates for repair or replacement. A standard claims form, which should be obtained from your insurance company, building society or broker as soon as possible after an incident, will also include questions about the age of each item and the price paid for it. You will also have to make a deduction for wear and tear, if you do not have a new-for-old policy. If you have any valuations for jewellery or antiques you should send these to back up your claim. Receipts for record players, televisions etc. may also be needed to support your claim.

Many people who have to make a claim for damage to their house wait until they have estimates from builders before making a claim. This is not wise as it can lead to delays in settling the claim when the work is finished. It is much better to put in an early claim with a provisional estimate for the damage. This also gives the insurance company an opportunity to come round and see the damage for themselves.

If it looks like being a large claim, valued at say several thousand pounds, the insurance company will want to send one of their own inspectors around as soon as possible. If you think you might have problems over the claim you should call in your own assessor to draw up a claim for you. Your insurance broker should be able to help you find an assessor. There is an approved association, called the Chartered Institute of Loss Adjusters who can be contacted at Mansfield House, 376 The Strand, London WC2R 0LR. Tel: 071-240 1496 or 071-836 6482.

Sometimes claims run into trouble. If you are not satisfied with the way a claim is being handled you should write to the chief executive of the company, setting out the problem briefly and clearly. If that does not help you will have to turn to one of the complaints bodies or trade associations listed below.

Extra insurance

In recent years insurance companies have developed several new forms of insurance cover for householders.

Personal legal expenses This can be added onto a contents policy for as little as £7.50 for the whole year: a few policies even include it automatically without extra charge. These policies offer a set amount of cover for the cost of pursuing a case against your neighbour, say, over a boundary dispute, your employer or against a shop. The policies also pay the costs of defending yourself, although they stop short of paying any fines for you.

Breakdown insurance There are one or two policies on the market that will help you out when you have one of those household emergencies such as a burst pipe. The most basic option available through an Italian company based in this country called Generali, enables you to phone Europ Assistance, who will put you in touch with a reputable tradesman in your area. Another policy, from Lombard Continental, goes further and pays the repair bill too, although it obviously costs more to buy this type of cover.

Specialist policies One example is pedal cycles. Contents policies will often only insure them up to £150. This is far too low for some bikes and their owners will need a specialist policy. There are some around, although you have to look out for the built-in depreciation with some of the policies, which would write a bike off within a few years! Musical instruments can be expensive to insure on a household insurance policy. Specialist policies will cover not only theft and damage, but also loss of use and hire of an alternative instrument.

People fortunate enough to own several works of art or expensive antiques should seek professional advice on their insurance and security needs. If these items add up to over 5% of the value of your contents policy, the insurance company will insist on imposing special conditions anyway.

Life cover

If you have a traditional building society repayment mortgage you will need to take out insurance to cover the outstanding loan if you should die. This means your dependents will not be left to pick up the tab of large monthly mortgage repayments or to face the grim alternative of moving out of the family home. A number of building societies or banks will insist you take out some form of life insurance to cover the loan even if you are single. This is another form of security against the loan as far as they are concerned.

You will usually be recommended to take out a mortgage protection policy. This is a type of term assurance and pays out a lump sum if you die before the end of the mortgage term. The policy will give life insurance cover for the person or persons who have taken out the mortgage. So, if it is only in one name, then the insurance policy will only be in that person's life. If the mortgage is in the name of a husband and wife, then so will the insurance policy be. In the case of joint policies, the insurance payout can be given on the death of either the first or second person. In the case of mortgage protection policies it is usual to opt for a so-called 'joint life first death' policy.

The most common type of mortgage protection policy is designed to reduce the insurance payout as the loan reduces. The technical term for this type of insurance is decreasing term assurance. As an alternative to this, some people opt for level term assurance where you match the amount of insurance to the initial size of the loan and it does not reduce as the loan is paid off. A decreasing term assurance policy is cheaper because the payouts get smaller the nearer you are to the end of the mortgage term. However, with a decreasing term insurance if you die there is not always a guarantee that the loan will be repaid in full as there is with a straightforward term policy.

TABLE 8
MONTHLY PREMIUMS FOR A LOAN OF £30,000 OVER 25 YEARS

	MORTGAGE PROTECTION		LEVEL TERM ASSURANCE	
	SMOKER	NON-SMOKER	SMOKER	NON-SMOKER
Man age 24	5.85	3.90	7.95	5.30
Couple, both age 24	8.37	5.33	11.82	7.88
Man age 38	14.70	9.84	21.42	14.28
Woman age 35	6.75	4.50	9.54	6.36

Based on the rates charged by one leading insurance company as at January 1991. You should check with your adviser to discuss the best policy and terms to suit your personal requirements.

As you will see from the tables, some insurance companies reduce the premiums for people who do not smoke or who have given up for at least a year. Some companies ask you to tell them if you start smoking again. If you take out a policy with an initial level of insurance of over £50,000, you may be asked to take a medical or your GP might be approached for a medical report. The level of insurance which triggers this off does vary from company to company and according to your age and state of health. If, after an examination, the insurance company thinks that you are a higher risk than usual, they may ask you to pay something extra. Most companies take a very similar attitude in such circumstances, although a few are noted for a more flexible approach. You should contact your local building society, bank or an insurance broker if you find yourself facing difficulties in getting life assurance.

If you have a pension mortgage you will be in a similar position. There is no insurance integral with the mortgage or the pension. However, if you are using a personal pension contract to back up your request for a home loan, then you can also take out term assurance through the pension plan to cover the loan. The great attraction of this is that you can get tax relief on the premiums at your highest rate of tax. The cost of your term insurance under a pension plan will be virtually identical to that for a repayment mortgage as shown in Table 8, except that you can deduct your highest marginal rate of tax from the monthly premiums as tax relief. So for the tax year 1988-9 you can save either 25% or 40% depending upon your income tax bracket.

If you have an endowment mortgage the protection element of the life insurance will be included, so there is no need to worry about any additional life insurance.

Addresses

Trade associations
Association of British Insurers, Aldermary House,
   Queen Street, London EC4N 1TP
British Insurance Brokers' Association, 14 Bevis Marks,
   London EC3A 7NT

Bodies handling complaints
Insurance Ombudsman Bureau, 31 Southampton Row,
   London WC1B 5HJ

Personal Insurance Arbitration Service, Institute of
   Arbitrators, 75 Cannon Street, London EC4
Consumer Enquiries Department, Lloyd's of London,
   Lime Street, London EC3M 7HA

CHAPTER FIVE: HOME IMPROVEMENTS

The perfect home does not exist. Most of us have to make do with what we can afford, while other constraints such as size and location will also limit our options when choosing a home.

Unless you start from scratch with an architect and unlimited funds at your disposal you are unlikely to get the house that you would ideally like to live in. But we can get a little bit closer to our dream house through home improvements. Nearly all houses can benefit from improvement, from the fifteenth century thatched barn to a modern three bedroom semi.

People improve their homes for many reasons: to make them more comfortable, cheaper to run, to give themselves more space, to provide special facilities for the disabled or the elderly, to improve the value of their property and in some cases just to stamp the owner's personal taste on an otherwise undistinguished property.

The need for home improvement may be obvious. According to the Department of Environment Survey on English housing conditions, out of the eighteen million dwellings in England for example, nearly four million needed major repairs or improvements. Nearly one and a half million were either unfit to live in or lacked a basic amenity such as an indoor lavatory or a bath.

While that is one end of the spectrum, the other is the home improvements that increase the comfort, security, running costs or appearance of otherwise perfectly sound homes.

The English House Condition Survey research concluded that we spend around six billion pounds a year on home improvements – a figure that does not include the unpaid do-it-yourself labour. If this is included the amount of money we spend rises to about eight billion pounds a year.

However, research from the Building Societies Association into home improvement habits suggests that home owners often spend money on the wrong things, lashing out thousands of pounds on stone cladding or replacement glazing when the house itself badly needs a new roof or damp proof course. Often the reason why money is spent on the wrong improvements instead of vital repairs and maintenance is that hard sell tactics are used to push double glazing or new kitchens. Essential repairs are down to the owners to do something off their own bat.

While much can be done to the average house to improve it, there is no point in spending too much money on home improvements – especially where they are not increasing the value of the property. Make sure that the home improvements you choose will give you some tangible benefit, such as greater comfort, convenience or security.

It may be more sensible, for example, to buy another house more suitable to your needs than to turn the present one inside out in the pursuit of the ideal home. Obviously, costs and convenience feature prominently in your ultimate decision. Many home owners may be stuck where they are, perhaps because they are disabled and need to be near relatives or they live in an area where houses are difficult to sell. Sometimes the benefits of major improvements go beyond the additional value they give to the house itself. It can be better in the long run to spend more than would otherwise be justified if you intend to stay where you are for the forseeable future.

What improvements?

Home improvements can be broadly put into two categories:
1. Basic necessary repairs
2. General improvements

The first category may involve work which is eligible for local authority grants. Such work can include the provision of basic amenities like a bath, indoor lavatory, heating and hot water to a wash hand basin and a kitchen sink. Grants may also be available for repairs and major improvements.

Grants for the provision of basic amenities are mandatory, which means that the local authority is obliged to provide money for this type of work. However, they may not have ready money available so check with your local authority. You may find you are placed on a waiting list.

If you live in a house which was built prior to 1919 you may qualify for repairs grants. These are at the discretion of the local authorities, many of which may have no money to pay for repairs. However, if you are buying or you live in a property which is in need of substantial repair or improvement it may still be worth getting in touch with your local authority to see if they do have any money available for grants.

The majority of home improvements fall into the second category and are aimed at making what is essentially a sound house more comfortable to live in. Home improvements can also improve the value of your house or make it more efficient to run or to work in.

Central heating

One of the most popular improvements is central heating. In terms of convenience and comfort this is one of the best improvements a home owner can make. In the long run it will pay for itself.

Look at your present hot water and heating system. It may be necessary to replace the entire plumbing system from the rising main right through the house. If you have lead plumbing – a major health hazard as well as being prone to leaks and bursts – you should be able to get a local authority grant to replace it.

In most houses the hot water system and the plumbing will be relatively modern. A central heating engineer or plumber will be able to tell you whether you need to replace it or not. Provided your plumbing system is sound, the next step is to decide which type of central heating you want to install.

There are four main options:

1. Gas fired central heating
2. Electric storage radiator system
3. Oil or solid fuel central heating
4. A hybrid system comprising several elements.

For most of us the choice is going to be between gas and electricity. For many years gas has been the cheaper of the two in terms of running costs. However, new electric storage systems running on cheap, off-peak electricity have brought the costs down substantially and there is now little difference between the two. Installation costs may be cheaper for an electrical system which does not require plumbing to individual radiators.

The most common form of electrical central heating system will use storage radiators which heat up during the night using cheap off-peak electricity and give out the heat when it is needed. Modern storage radiators are slim and more flexible in their operation than the older models.

The hot water will be heated using a separate immersion system. Again this is different from the old immersion heater and involves two heating elements in a much larger hot water tank. The bottom element will heat the tank during the night using off-peak electricity, while the upper element can be turned on to provide extra hot water quickly.

Gas central heating has advantages for large homes where the costs of electrical systems start to increase compared to gas systems. With adequate heating controls a gas system can be more flexible too.

Oil and solid fuel systems are primarily of use where gas is unavailable and an electrical system is uneconomic – a large country house, for example. Oil has fallen considerably in price and is now much more competitive than it used to be. However, the price is volatile and you should bear this in mind when you think about installing it.

Solid fuel is best used for background heating in a hybrid system which involves other sources of heat – electricity or log fires perhaps.

Both oil and solid fuel systems need a lot of maintenance – solid fuel systems require daily attention – and space for storing the fuel. If you have the space a solid fuel bunker can be built which feeds directly into the heating system. However, in most cases a solid system will involve daily or twice-daily trips to the bunker to stoke up the boiler.

For the average three bedroom house installation costs for a gas or electric heating and hot water system are about £3,500-£4,500. If the plumbing and hot water system needs replacing this will cost up to another £1,800. These estimates are based on prices in the spring of 1991 and you should always check in advance the total costs before embarking on a major programme of installation repair.

Remember that installing central heating is only one part of the story. You can make your heating system much more efficient and cheaper to run by making sure you have adequate controls. A timer on the boiler and thermostats fitted to each radiator will ensure that the house is heated to the temperature you want when you want. If radiator thermostats are too costly, you can use a room thermostat but this is much less flexible and efficient. A thermostat fitted to the hot water tank will ensure that you are heating the hot water to exactly the temperature you need. Make sure, too, that your hot water tank is well insulated.

Insulation, double glazing and replacement windows

There is little point in improving your heating system if you are going to spend a fortune heating the air above your house. Insulating your home is the next priority.

About 25% of the heat is lost through the roof space in an uninsulated home. The rest is lost through the walls (35%), the floor (15%) and windows and doors (25%).

The roof is the easiest and cheapest problem to deal with. The loft should be insulated with at least four inches of a recommended material – usually glass fibre blanket or a loose fill material. Make sure, however, that there is adequate ventilation to the roof space when you do the work.

A grant is available from your local authority for up to 90% of the cost of the work up to a maximum of £95 but under new government rules due to be introduced in Spring 1987 only if you are receiving Housing Benefit or Supplementary Benefit and if your loft insulation does not come up to the recommended standard. If you do qualify for a grant, the local authority will require you to insulate your water tank and pipes at the same time. Do not insulate under the tank. Heat rising from the house will stop it from freezing in winter.

While heat losses from doors and windows can be stemmed with efficient draught proofing, many older properties could benefit from replacement windows. This can be very expensive – several thousand pounds for an average house – but the benefits come in lower heating bills, a draught-free home, reduced noise from outside and usually an increase in the value of your house.

Replacement windows, as the phrase suggests, involves taking out existing windows and replacing them with new ones. New window frames may be treated hardwood, aluminium or thermoplastic. In any event the new windows should need little maintenance and will provide improved insulation.

Double glazing may or may not involve replacing the windows. Many of the cheaper systems and DIY packages on the market are actually secondary glazing systems, where a second layer of glass is applied over the existing windows. Such systems can be very effective and cheap to install.

If your windows are in a poor state, however, it may be better to replace the lot. A double glazing system will be more expensive but will, if correctly installed, vastly improve the insulation and comfort of your home.

One of the problems with double glazing is the high pressure sales tactics that some firms use to persuade you to buy. Apart from the use of door to door cold calling tactics, salesmen often try to pressure you by offering discounts if you 'close the deal' there and then. Be sure you understand exactly what you are paying for and how much it is going to cost. Ask whether the salesman is providing you with an estimate or a quotation. Remember that there is a cooling off period of five days after you have signed the contract, which means you can change your mind up to seven days later by simply writing and cancelling the agreement.

Wall insulation is generally only worthwhile if you have cavity walls. In general, homes built prior to 1930 will have solid walls and can only be insulated by drylining the inside or applying insulation to the outside. Either way the process is very expensive and will probably not justify the cost.

Cavity wall insulation for homes built after 1930 can reduce heating bills dramatically. Installation is best done by a specialist contractor using special machinery. Three types of material are commonly used: urea formaldehyde foam, blown mineral fibre and polystyrene beads or granules.

Remember that problems can occur if you do fill a cavity wall. In particular, ask a specialist to check that there is no rubble or cement trapped in the cavity which indirectly could lead to condensation. Cavity walls by themselves are intended to provide some insulation and filling them can create more problems than it solves if the job is not done correctly. The experts tend to recommend a loose-fill material such as mineral fibre or polystyrene granules as these can be removed if problems subsequently occur. The cost of installation for an average three bedroom semi in spring 1991 start at around £250 for UF foam, rising to around £480 for polystyrene beads.

Remember too that cavities in timber frame walls should never be filled. Modern timber frame construction is one of the most well-insulated forms of building and should not need any further insulation.

Kitchens

There is probably no home improvement that causes quite so much anguish as putting in a new kitchen. The engine room of the house, the kitchen is an area in virtually constant use and even minor disruptions can upset the household routine.

How much more so then, than when you are having the whole thing ripped out and replaced? There is no easy solution to the problem of reducing the chaos that a kitchen refit will inevitably involve. Replacing an old kitchen with a new one requires such a diversity of sources of supply and labour as well as management and planning skills that it is a wonder the job ever gets done.

Apart from obtaining all the equipment – units, worktops, white goods, electrics, plumbing and decorating materials and flooring, you have to make sure the right people are available at the right time. You'll need an electrician to install the new electrical circuits, a plumber to handle the plumbing, plus an assortment of builders and their mates to erect the units, fit the worktops and complete a variety of jobs such as tiling, painting, laying lino or floor tiles and putting in new light fittings.

Putting in a new kitchen may involve you in major building work: taking down walls, moving doorways, putting in new windows or even building a new extension, and this will inevitably add to the cost. Specialist kitchen fitting companies may take on the basic building work but they are more likely to want you to get the work done before they start.

How much you will pay is rather like asking how long is a piece of string. The sky is the limit if you want the last word in kitchen technology replete with every conceivable modern gadget available. At the other end of the scale a kitchen refit by a specialist firm is unlikely to cost less than £2,800 to £3,300. A larger kitchen with double oven hob, dishwasher, double sink and drainer, washing machine and tumble dryer and fridge freezer could cost around £5,300 to £7,850 if you go for a more up-market range of fittings, according to the National Home Improvement Council figures.

If the comprehensive kitchen fitting specialist is too expensive, you could either ask the suppliers of the kitchen units if they will fit them or if they know of someone who specialises in fitting kitchens. A builder may take on the job but kitchens, as we have seen, require such diverse skills that many builders would not be interested in the job. The third option is to do it yourself. This will depend very much on how you rate your DIY skills and how much time you have to do the work.

A modern and attractive kitchen is undoubtedly a strong selling point if you ever put your home on the market. However, it is difficult to quantify exactly how much a new kitchen will add to your home's value. When considering a new kitchen you should bear in mind that it is primarily for your own use and not just a way of improving the value of your home.

Bathrooms

Bathrooms present fewer problems. They are usually a more straightforward job of refitting existing facilities that should not be beyond the capability of the average plumber. Many people, if they are contemplating having their bathroom refitted, will want a separate shower installed or a shower over the bath.

There are numerous companies which specialise in fitting shower units, some of whom have in the past been accused of less than scrupulous sales tactics.

Problems with showers can occur where there is little pressure in the hot water system, perhaps because the water storage tank is on the same level as the bathroom. In such a case a pumped shower system should be installed which will supply water under pressure. Showers can be run off the existing hot water system but many new showers use an electric water heater. The efficiency of these systems varies but check that yours is properly installed by a qualified fitter.

Extensions and conversions

You may decide that your house is too small for your present needs, that the rooms are inconveniently laid out or that there is underused space which could be made habitable. In this case you may consider either adding an extension onto the house or converting the loft or the cellar into habitable rooms.

Extensions may take the form of an add-on conservatory which can be built on the side of the house and which forms an extension of the living or dining-room area. This is a comparatively cheap way of doing it. There are a number of standard glazed extensions and conservatories of this type on the market, ranging from a simple lean-to greenhouse style model to grandiose Victorian or Edwardian replica conservatories.

Once the concrete base for the extension has been laid the extension itself can be erected in a day or two. Prices vary but a small glazed extension could start at around £1,300 plus building costs.

A more permanent extension to the house will be more expensive and will normally involve calling in the builders. Depending on the size of the proposed extension you may have to get planning permission from the local authority. You may also have to get clearance under building regulations. However, new rules for planning permission and building regulations are much more relaxed and you may find that you do not need official approval.

In any event you would be well advised to instruct an architect to draw up the plans for the proposed addition and to advise you on local planning requirements before proceeding with any work. Some firms which specialise in extensions and conversions do the planning work as part of their overall service. In some rare cases local authorities have ordered improvements to be removed or the property restored to its original state where work is in breach of local planning or building regulations; for example where the property is a listed building.

Home improvements

TYPE OF IMPROVEMENT	ESTIMATED COST	BENEFITS
Central heating	£3,500-£4,500	Will almost certainly add to the value of your home and is one of the most cost-effective improvements you can make. Overall heating bills may got up depending on what your heating arrangements are now but in terms of the amount of heating you get for your money central heating is the most efficient way of doing it.
Insulation: a) roof	£100-£120 plus labour	Will cut down heating bills dramatically and will certainly pay for itself within a year or two. If you get a grant to install or top up your insulation the cost can be negligible.
b) cavity walls	£350-£700	Will pay for itself in reduced heating bills within a few years. May add to value of house.
c) double glazing	£6,500 upwards	Probably not worthwhile if your windows are already in good condition. If they need replacing then the additional cost of double glazing will be partially recouped from lower bills. May contribute to an increase in the value of your house. Figures quoted are for a DIY secondary glazing system to a full replacement window installation.
d) Secondary glazing	£100-£600	Cost per window depending on size and whether it is a professional job or DIY.

Kitchen refit	£2,500 upwards	May contribute to an increase in the value of your house. Will almost certainly increase its selling potential. However, it is easy to overspend and buyers may have different ideas about their ideal kitchen.
Conversions and extensions: a) pre-fab conservatory	£1,500 upwards	In general a brick and block built extension is likely to increase the value of your house while a prefabricated extension will not.
b) built extension	£5,500 upwards	

Remember that the first and best reason for undertaking home improvements is to make your home more suited to your requirements, more comfortable to live in or cheap to run. The real benefits of improvements come from the satisfaction that you will get from them and this must be taken into account when you are deciding whether or not to improve your property.

Home improvements may produce an increase in the value of your property but this may not be matched pound for pound with the money you spend – especially in the short term. Some improvements will probably not add as much to the value of your property as you paid for them. Unless you are proposing to stay put for the foreseeable future do not spend more than your property is worth on the market.

So if you bought your house for £30,000 and similar houses are now selling for £45,000, there is no point in spending more than £15,000 unless you intend to stay put long enough to recoup your investment. If you spend more, then you will have paid more for your property than you would get back if you sold it.

Choosing a builder

The Federation of Master Builders runs a guarantee scheme called the National Register of Warranted Builders. If you use a builder who is registered under the scheme and opt for the warranty you will get a gurantee that any additional costs incurred if the original builder ceases trading before completing the work will be paid for by the Federation up to a maximum of £10,000. The completion work will be undertaken by another building of the client's choice.

You are protected against defects through faulty materials or workmanship for two years after the works have been completed. Defects can be reported to the Registrar of the scheme and if agreed will be put right at no expense to you, even if the builder has ceased trading in the meantime.

In the event of a dispute the scheme provides a free conciliation and arbitration service. The cost of the scheme is 1% of the contract price, including VAT and it applies to jobs with a ceiling of £75,000, including VAT.

Details of the National Register of Warranted Builders can be obtained from: The Federation of Master Builders, Gordon Fisher House, 33 John Street, London WC1N 2BB. Tel: 071-242 7583

Home security

With burglaries on the increase one of the most cost effective home improvements you can make is to increase the security of your home. As nearly half of all burglaries are through windows make sure an intruder cannot get in by this route. You can fit a variety of different locks, most of which require a special key to open them. Even if the burglar breaks a window pane the lock will prevent him from opening the window and most burglars will not climb through a broken window pane. Securing your windows is not expensive, with a maximum cost including fitting charges of around £12. The table shows the choice and cost range.

Entrance doors can be protected by installing five-lever mortise deadlocks which fit into the door itself. Rim locks which screw onto the door are useful but more effective as an addition rather than instead of a mortise deadlock. Fitting two mortice deadlocks to your door will also provide you with additional security. To stop an intruder forcing the hinges of the door you can fit special bolts. These hinge bolts automatically fit into recesses in the hinged edge of the door when it is closed and prevent the door being forced.

Additional door security can include a door chain which will prevent the door being opened more than a few inches and a door viewer which will enable you to see who is at the door before opening it. Rear entrances or rarely used doors can be fitted with security bolts which are locked with a special key.

Table: Securing Your Windows

TYPE OF SECURITY			HIGH £	MEDIUM £	ECONOMY £
SASH WINDOWS	A	Push to lock	5.50		
	B	Quick fit		4.75	
	C	Dual screws			1.80
WOOD HINGED WINDOWS	D	Snap action	5.20		
	E	Quick fit		4.15	
	F	Easy fit			1.90
METAL HINGED WINDOWS	G	Turn catch lock	7.20		
	H	Quick fit		4.75	
	I	Handle lock			3.25
Average DIY cost for 9 windows			53.70	40.95	20.85
Estimated fitting cost*			45.00	40.00	22.50
Total fitted price			98.70	80.95	43.35

NB: On poorly fitting and larger windows two locks should be fitted. Cost may vary. Readers are advised to shop around.

Patio doors should be fitted with locks top and bottom so that the door cannot be lifted off its track or opened by breaking the glass. French windows benefit from similar treatment with security bolts fitted to the top and bottom.

For really high security,doors and doorframes can be reinforced or replaced with special models. This may be necessary,for example, if you live in an area where forced entrance is common. The total bill for securing your doors will vary between around £30 and £65.

Alarm systems can be fitted to your home which will give greater security. For this you will need the advice of an expert. Your local Crime Prevention Officer will be able to help. Remember that some insurers now offer discounts on home

Table: Securing Your Doors

TYPE OF SECURITY	HIGH £	MEDIUM £	ECONOMY £
A1 5-lever mortise deadlock BS 3621	35.00		
A2 5-lever mortise deadlock		18.00	18.00
B Door chain/door limiter	1.70	1.70	1.70
C Door viewer	3.00	3.00	
D Door hinge bolts (pair)	6.00		
E Security bolts (pair)	6.00		
Total DIY cost	51.70	22.70	19.70
Estimated fitting cost*	27.00	16.50	14.00
Total fitted price	78.70	39.20	33.70

* These costs may vary. Readers are advised to shop around.

contents insurance if you have adequate home security or a burglar alarm system. If you do want to fit a burglar alarm consult your insurer. Most insurance companies recommend that work is carried out by members of the National Supervisory Council of Intruder Alarms: Head office, St Ives Road, Maidenhead, Berkshire. They will be able to supply you with a list of local installers.

Finance

Home improvements are never cheap and what started as a minor job can all too soon mount up to a major expense. While you can reduce the costs by doing some or all of the work yourself, this may not be practical. You may not have the time or the skill to install central heating, build a loft conversion or refit a kitchen. Surprisingly, the majority of home improvements are financed out of the householder's own resources. However, if you need to borrow money it pays to spend a little time checking out the options.

Specialist providers of home improvements such as replacement windows, central heating or kitchen refits may provide their own finance. Borrowing the money yourself from a bank or a building society will usually be cheaper.

There should be no strings which tie you to the home improvement company's finance, such as discounts conditional on accepting their finance. Such conditions are illegal and you should be wary of anyone who attempts to impose them.

Building societies and banks will lend money for home improvements. However, you will need to give the bank or building society rough estimates of work to be done and invoices on completion. In some cases, they may even send a member of staff to ensure that the works have been completed. Tax relief on the interest on loans raised to improve your property was abolished in the 1988 Budget as the government argued the system was being abused and the money borrowed in this way was fuelling general consumer expenditure.

How much you can afford to borrow depends on your ability to repay the loan. Building societies used to be restricted to lending money using the house as security for the loan. This meant that mortgage borrowing plus home improvement loans should not add up to more than the value of the house. Now building societies, like banks, can make unsecured loans. However, it would be very unwise for a householder considering home improvement work to borrow more than the house is worth unless they have a substantial income or other assets to give them a cash cushion.

Remember that there is no point in spending more money on home improvements than you are likely to get back if you sell the house, unless there are special reasons why you want to stay in a particular house or there are special facilities that you need.

In general terms, most home improvements will be reflected in the value of the house. The better the condition you keep your property in the more likely you are to find a buyer when you come to sell and the better the price you will get.

Having said that, the three most important factors in valuing a house – as the old valuer's adage goes – are: location, location and location. It does not matter if your three bed semi is done out like the palace of Versailles. If the local price for that property is between £25,000 and £30,000 the most you are likely to get is the top of that price range.

Anyone considering paying more will probably be looking at homes in a different and more expensive area. As a rule of thumb add up the costs of the proposed improvements to the price you paid for your house. If the total comes to more than the current price that similar houses are going for, then you are probably spending too much on your property.

However, if you live in an area where house prices are rising, it may be worth spending the money now on the basis that prices will have increased sufficiently by the time you sell to cover the cost of the improvements. How long that will be will depend on how much you spend and what happens to house prices. Remember, too, that the cost of home improvements is unlikely to get cheaper, although competition in some fields has reduced the relative costs of double glazing and other improvements.

What do we spend our money on?

The most recent Building Society Association survey into home improvement habits of owner occupiers threw up some surprising results. In general the survey showed that most home improvement work is financed by home owners themselves with two-thirds of home improvements requiring no borrowing by the householder. Of those who did borrow, 17% went to their building society, 1% took out a mortgage from their bank while a further 9% took out a personal bank loan.

The most popular type of home improvement that home owners carried out the survey showed was the installation of double glazing and had been done by 36% of the survey sample over the previous five years. Next came the kitchen refit which had been done by 35% over the last five years. New roofs and damp proof courses trailed at around 9% and 7% respectively.

Improvements undertaken over the last five years

Improvement	Per cent
Double glazing or new windows	36
Refit kitchen	35
Refit bathroom	24
Install central heating	20
Rewire	19

Build extension or conversion	16
New roof	9
Install cavity wall insulation	9
Install damp proof course	7

(Figures show the percentage of respondents to the Building Societies Association's survey who have installed a particular improvement over the last five years.
Source: Housing and Savings 1986, Technical Report and Tables – BSA 1986.)

Planning permission and Building Regulations

Recent changes to the rules surrounding planning permission should simplify matters considerably for home owners planning improvements or extensions to their property. In general terms, you will not need planning permission if your proposals fall into the categories of permitted development. No planning permission will be needed if the extension does not exceed 70 cubic metres in volume or 15% of the original house on houses, except for terraced ones where the figures are respectively 50 cubic metres and 10%.

Extensions should not be higher than the highest part of the original house. If the house fronts on to a highway then the extension should not project forward any further than the existing frontage. If the extension is within two metres of a boundary wall it should not be over four metres high.

New rules allow the insertion of windows, including dormer windows, or the alteration or enlargement of existing windows without planning permission, provided the resulting structure does not exceed two metres in height or in the case of dormer windows would alter more than half of the surface area of the existing roof face.

The rules have also been relaxed for those who wish to build porches, install satellite antennae and lay patios. These will no longer require planning permission unless they exceed the generous sizes specified in the rules. Stricter rules still outstanding natural beauty or National Parks and to listed buildings.

If you are in doubt over your plans consult your local planning officer. The local planning department will probably be listed in the telephone directory. If not, the town hall will be able to give you the number. Remember, there is no point in trying to ignore or get around planning restrictions. You could find yourself having to take down the extension if it is discovered and, let's face it, brick and mortar are not easy to hide. The Department of the Environment and Welsh Office provide a handy free leaflet called Planning: A Householder's Guide, which is well worth reading.

Building Regulations

Building Regulations are primarily intended to ensure that the work you carry out is safe. Recent changes to the Building Regulations mean that the building control officers take a more liberal approach to the rules. They have to be satisfied that you meet the general requirements of the Regulations rather than demanding that things be done in a particular way.

There are accepted ways of doing things, however, and it will be easier to get the work approved by the Building Control Officer if you follow one of these methods. Improvements which have to meet Building Regulations include brick built extensions, loft conversions, major structural alterations and changes to drainage and cavity wall insulation. The changes to the Regulations also mean that many home improvements are exempt from Building Regulations. These include garages and conservatories up to 30 square metres in area porches and greenhouses while some requirements are less stringent than before.

Application for planning permission and Building Regulation approval is made to the respective departments of the local authority. Applications for planning permission will need full plans and will go before a planning committee if objections have been received, from your neighbours, for example. You should receive a decision within eight weeks. For the Building Regulations you have the choose of either lodging full plans for the proposed works or giving a 'building notice'. A qualified architect or a building surveyor will be able to help you with your plans or the building notice.

While some home improvement firms may offer a comprehensive service, including all planning and building regulation approval, you may need to employ your own professionals. The RIBA can give you the names of local architects who can carry out home improvement work.

RIBA REGIONAL OFFICES

Eastern, London,
South West Regions
All are based at RIBA Headquarters
66 Portland Place, London W1N 4AD
(071-580 5533)

East Midlands Region
3 St James's Terrace, Nottingham NG1 6FW
(0602 413650)

Northern Region
6 Higham Place, Newcastle upon Tyne
NE1 8AF   (091-232 4436)

North West Region
44-46 King Street, Knutsford, Cheshire
WA16 6HJ   (0565 52927)

Southern Region
St Pauls Gate, Cross Street, Winchester, Hants
SO23 8SZ   (0962 60095)

South East Region
4 St John's Road, Tunbridge Wells, Kent
TN4 9NP   (0892 515878)

West Midlands Region
Birmingham and Midland Institute
Margaret Street, Birmingham B3 3SP
(021-233 2321)

Yorkshire Region
8 Woodhouse Square, Leeds LS3 1AD
(0532 456250)

Scotland
Royal Incorporation of Architects in Scotland
15 Rutland Square, Edinburgh EH1 2BE
(031-229 7205)

Wales
Society of Architects in Wales
75a Llandennis Road, Rhydypennau, Cardiff
CF2 6EE   (0222 762215)

Ulster
Royal Society of Ulster Architects
2 Mount Charles, Belfast BT7 1NZ
(0232 223760)

The Royal Institution of Chartered Surveyors (RICS) will be able to give you the names of building surveyors in your area. RICS: 12 Great George Street, London SW1, Tel: 071-222 7000.

CHAPTER SIX:
TIPS FOR
HASSLED HOMEOWNERS

1. Paint power

By far the quickest and cheapest way to transform and revitalise a room is with a dash of colour. If your bank balance has shrunk into insignificance after paying for the move then simply getting your fingers painting may be just the tonic your new home needs.

● **Enlarge a room**
Use light colours on walls and ceiling to give an instant facelift and the appearance of greater size.

● **Ceiling too high**
Dark colours on the walls will immediately give the room a more cosy feel. Keep the ceiling light, otherwise you will get a claustrophobic feeling.

● **Cold north-facing rooms**
Add a touch of warmth with sunny yellows, apricots or even pinks and reds.

● **Intimate interiors**
Rich colours, such as claret red, chestnut, deep blue or velvety green, can be used to create a sumptuous atmosphere in dining-rooms.

● **All-over facelift**
Cream, white, beige, grey or even some of those pastel tinged whites may be a cliché of good taste, but they provide a marvellous background for that hodge podge of furniture, pictures, cushions etc. you've amassed over the years.

Paint choice

Once you've chosen the colour, the next step is to pick the right type of paint to achieve the effect you are seeking. There are nearly as many different types as there are soap powders, so here's a brief run-down:

● **Oil-based paints**
These give the best finish but are the hardest for the amateur to apply. Professional decorators usually prefer to use gloss

oil-based paints for woodwork or covering metal as it gives a hard-wearing, high-sheen finish, which is much easier to clean than the finish provided by water-based emulsion paints. For this reason it is the preferred choice of the professional decorator for windowsills, in bathrooms and kitchens, on metal cabinets. Gloss tends to intensify the colour of the paint so bear that in mind when choosing colours. Eggshell finishes are usually used on inside walls and again provide a fine finish but need to be skilfully applied. Prices vary enormously, depending on where you buy, but £7.55 for 2½ litres is about average.

● **Emulsion paints**
These are often used for walls and ceilings; they are water-based and are not as hard-wearing as oil-based paints. But they are much easier to handle, quicker to dry and don't need thinning or an undercoat – though usually several coats of emulsion will be needed to get a good finish. You can usually choose between a matt finish or a slight sheen. Again, it is worth shopping around, but prices average out at about £4.50 a litre.

● **Non-drip paint**
This is the do-it-yourselfer's dream, being easy to apply and less liable to drip or run. It has a good tough finish and so can be used instead of an oil-based gloss. Most big manufacturers, like Crown, sell non-drip paints. Prices start at £4.99 for 2½ litres in emulsion, £6.49 for 2½ litres gloss.

● **Wood stains**
These can be either oil or water-based and come in a range of colours. Mainly used for floors, furniture, picture frames and sometimes on stripped door and window frames. Sterling Roncraft do a good range of colours at £4.99 for 750 ml.

● **Textured emulsion**
This is often used to disguise bad plasterwork and uneven surfaces and is, on the whole, not to be recommended unless you are desperate. It always looks as if it is disguising something unattractive and is exceedingly difficult both to clean and to remove.

2. Home decorating tips

1. Go slowly. Don't be rushed or bullied into decisions before you're ready.
2. Remember, it's *your* house, you are the one who has got to live with the decorations. Have confidence in your own taste and preferences.
3. Successful schemes have not only to look good – they must *work*. Try and be clear in your mind about what the function of each room is. Choose fabrics, surfaces and a mood that fits this. Besides pretty pictures, plants and lovely fabrics, you must have lights that work, sofas that are comfortable and shelves on which to store things.
4. Be frank about the problems. If a room is really dark try and decide carefully whether you are (a) going to make it look lighter or (b) turn it into a magical evening room, full of dark enchantment.
5. Don't be afraid to experiment. Get as many swatches and samples as you can. Test them against the light and furnishings in the room. If you like something, do go ahead with it even if no one else has done it before.
6. Do remember that a colour scheme doesn't work in isolation – it has to be a background for your possessions and furniture.
7. Take into account what is appropriate for your house or room. Unless you have a very sure eye indeed it is much safer to go with, rather than against, the prevailing style. Don't go for chandeliers and too much country house chintz in a bungalow. In small rooms try to choose colours that will enlarge and furniture that is in scale.
8. Don't be afraid to copy an idea you like. By the time it is in your house and surrounded by your own objects, it will look very different from the original.
9. Remember that successful cheating is what a lot of successful interior design is about. Illusions of space, of warmth, of light, of airiness, can all be created if that's what you want.
10. Don't assume that because a room is officially called a dining-room that is what it has to be for all time. It may work better for you as a study or you can turn part of the kitchen into an eating area. Similarly bedrooms can

double as studies, studies as dining-rooms, halls as workrooms. Be prepared to look and think afresh.

3. Theft proofing

Even if you are insured to the hilt, you'll have to foot the first part of the bill to replace your stolen goods, not to mention the mental anguish and distress. There are all sorts of preventative measures you can take which fall short of paying out around £800 for a complete burglar alarm system.

● Fit window locks on ground floor windows and vulnerable upstairs ones which can, for instance, be reached from a flat roof. Polycell and Ingersoll make locks from £3.

● Five lever security mortice locks for front and back door (British Standard 3621) start at around £18. They must be fitted securely to a stout door. There is no point having an impenetrable lock on a door which can easily be kicked in. Solid wood doors cost about £80, but then you will probably need a carpenter to fit them.

● Security chains cost about £3 to £4 and viewers which allow you to see the person outside the door start at around £3.50. There is a device on the market called the Security Vision Nameplate. It looks like a nameplate but gives you a clear three inches to spy on your caller (£7.95).

● To stop anyone climbing up your drain pipes, paint them with a non-drying paint such as Deter (£14.20 per litre).

● One or two timers fitted to table lamps set to go on and off at different times during the evening can help to give the impression that someone is at home. Try fitting another timer to a radio for added authenticity.

● You can also buy lights which sense the heat of human bodies and light up when anyone approaches. But while a straightforward timer costs around £17, one of these infra-red lights would set you back over £50.

● Double glazing installed for its heat-saving or noise-blocking properties may also act as a deterrent to burglars. But laminated glass is even more effective. This is glass with a plastic layer in the middle which holds the glass in place when it is attacked. A panel one metre square would cost about £38 but fitting would be extra.

● You can get the crime prevention officer from your local police station to survey your house absolutely free. He will make realistic recommendations about ways to tighten your security.

● It also costs nothing to join a local Neighbourhood Watch Scheme, or talk to the crime prevention officer about starting one up if there is not already one running in your area.

● And in case all this fails – it is a wise precaution to mark your post code on your valuable possessions with ultra-violet invisible ink. Both the Berol and Topline packs cost under £2 and also give you warning stickers to stick on your windows.

4. Cutting out the middle men

You do not have to wait for the sales to obtain bargains. You can go directly to the factory gates of a host of manufacturers and pick up old stock or slight seconds at between a third to a half off the normal shop prices.

These factory shops are a part of Midlands culture which may seem impenetrable to outsiders. But an enterprising Southerner, Gillian Cutress, who discovered factory shops when she was doing geological work in Nottinghamshire is writing a series of guides to these treasure troves.

So far she has produced guides to Derbyshire and Nottinghamshire, Leicestershire and Staffordshire. They tell you what the factories sell, when they are open and exactly how to get to them. The Derbyshire and Nottinghamshire guide, for instance, has fifty-eight entries and includes factories which sell pine furniture, crystal glasses, household linens, curtains, cushion covers, blinds and wallpapers.

The next guides will be on Yorkshire where there are great bargains in bedding, duvets, pillows and furnishing velvet; and Worcestershire where you can find carpets and glasswear including glass lampshades.

You do have to inspect the goods for any faults, but these are often minute. The stock at these factory shops varies from day to day, so you can never be sure exactly what you will find, but this does add a sense of adventure to an otherwise mundane shopping expedition.

Many of the factories will arrange tours and let you watch

the factory at work. The Factory guides are published by Gillian Cutress herself who is currently updating the existing books. They are available from local bookshops and W.H. Smith in the areas covered and from factory shops. They cost around £2 each.

5. Waste not, want not

It is extremely difficult to save money by re-cycling waste, but it can be done. You will also get a glow of satisfaction knowing that you are conserving the earth's resources. Reverse vending machines have been installed in six Birmingham supermarkets and another in Northampton. These machines accept empty aluminium cans. In return you get tokens or coins.

You can also get about 1p per can for sacks of aluminium cans from East Anglian Metals which will collect them when you have filled a minimum of thirty sacks. Each sack, which they will provide, can hold at least two hundred squashed and washed cans. So thirty full sacks should produce £60.

Can makers have installed special skips in various city-centre locations to collect any type of can. They give £8 to a local charity for every tonne of metal collected plus a bonus of £4 for every skip with more than one tonne in it.

There is no limit to the sorts of rubbish that different charities will accept. The Cats Protection League will even take cat combings which they can sell to manufacturers of a vaccine for those suffering from feline allergies.

More information contact Friends of the Earth, 377 City Road, London EC1V 1NA. Telephone 01-837 0731.

6. Cheaper insurance

Once you have tightened up on security and joined the local Neighbourhood Watch Scheme, you may be tempted to dash for one of the household contents insurance policies that offer discounts for security. But beware, you may find that some of the standard policies still work out cheaper than the so-called discount model. That said, the discounts are still worth investigating.

Norwich Union offer a 5% discount for proper door and window locks, a further 5% discount for a burglar alarm approved by the National Security Council for Intruder Alarms (NSCIA), and an additional 2½% discount for joining a police approved Neighbourhood Watch Scheme. This adds up to a maximum discount of 12½%. With Royal Insurance good locks alone do not qualify for a discount, but anyone with a full security set-up including tough locks and a burglar alarm gets a 15% discount. The alarm alone qualifies for a 5% discount. If you join a Neighbourhood Watch you receive a further 5% discount, making a maximum discount of 20%.

Other schemes are aimed at particular sorts of households. Legal and General's Homesafe policy is restricted to those with less than £5,000 worth of high risk items such as TV, video, cameras, furs, cash and jewellery. There are no vigorous security requirements beyond fitting good locks to doors and vulnerable windows. But there are other restrictions. The house or flat must normally be occupied during the day, and anyone who has made a claim on a contents policy within the past three years will not qualify for the discount. The discounts vary from 13% in low risk rural areas to 20% in high risk areas.

Sun Alliance's Firemark policy is targeted at the wealthier end of the market with a minimum sum assured of £20,000. There is a standard 10% discount for adequate security. There are two rates of cover, one for standard items and a much higher one for high risk items such as furs, clocks and jewellery. However, at least these are also covered for loss outside the home, known in the trade as an 'all-risks' policy. For instance, in central London, a highly rated area, high risk items are charged at £40 per £1,000 and standard items at £14 per £1,000.

The rates in the most highly rated areas under these four discount schemes vary from £9.60 to £13.12 per £1,000 even with the maximum discount. The TSB, which has no discount scheme, charges £9 per £1,000, so it may be cheaper than these so-called 'cut price' rates.

Your home might be in the most highly rated area with one company but not with another. So it is impossible to compare rates without specifying a location. A good insurance broker who specialises in home contents insurance will probably earn his or her keep. Otherwise, I'm afraid that boring old maxim 'shop around' applies here more and more as policies become more complicated and finely graded.

7. Helping hand for leaseholders

If you are buying a flat, this will be leasehold. That means you are buying the right to live there for as many years as the lease has left to run. You may think that buying somewhere with a 60 year lease is plenty long enough for your needs. But you may have difficulties when you come to sell. Building societies are not keen to lend money on any property whose lease will have only twenty years left after the mortgage is repaid. As the number of years reduces past a certain point, the value of your property will start going down as it becomes unmortgageable. One solution is to try and buy out the lease if the freeholder agrees. If for example there are about fifty years left to run, try offering twelve times the annual rent to buy it out. This will substantially increase the value of the property if it had a short lease. For example, on a house in London you could boost the current value by around 50% if the lease has forty years left.

8. Heat conservation

It is such a waste of money to let expensive warmth seep out through cracks. You can buy sticky-sided rolls of foam to put around doors and windows for a snug draught-proof fit. Fix a flap over the letter-box and construct make-shift double-glazing with cling-film.

If you have central heating there are a host of tricks to make it work more efficiently for you. Turning up the room thermostat will not heat up the room any faster. The way to do that is to raise the boiler thermostat, but beware as that will use more fuel. Have the boiler serviced regularly otherwise it will become inefficient rather like an old car engine.

To make the room radiators work efficiently put kitchen foil, shiny side out, onto outside walls behind them. Have long curtains behind them, never in front and fit small shelves above the radiators to deflect the rising warm air towards the

117

centre of the room. Fit individual thermostats to the radiators so each room can be controlled separately. Bedrooms do not need to be kept as warm as living rooms.

Think about all the hot water you use in washing up. Age Concern, in their free fact sheet 'Help With Heating', recommend that the washing-up is saved for a once a day blitz. Do not wash under a running tap and rinse the dishes in cold water. Always repair dripping hot taps quickly.

9. What's watt.

The first step towards to controlling your electricity bills is knowing how much power you are using. Most of us have little or no idea. London Electricity Board has come up with the statistics to help you do your sums. You can toast seventy slices of bread or make thirty-five cups of tea for one unit of electricity. The figures show you the number of units gobbled up by most household appliances and can be used to adjust your fuel consumption.

Battery charger(12V) 30 hours' charging - 1 unit.

Single overblanket all night for 1 week - 2 units.

Single underblanket 1½-2 hours' use each night for 1 week - less than one unit.

Can opener several thousand cans opened - 1 unit.

Carving knife over 200 joints carved - 1 unit.

Coffee mill 50kgs (110lbs) coffee ground - 1 unit.

Coffee percolator 75 cups of coffee made - 1 unit.

Contact grill more than 25 medium well-done steaks cooked - 1 unit.

Cooker one week's meals for average family - about 17 units.

Cooker hob bacon and egg breakfast for 4 - less than ½ unit.
Radiant boiling ring chicken stew for 4 - less than ½ unit.

Conventional oven 24 scones - 1 unit.

Fan oven 48 meringues - 1 unit.

Grill ½kg (1lb) pork sausages - less than ½ unit.

Cooker hood 10 hours' use - 1 unit.

Crêpe maker 139 crepes made at one session - 1 unit.

Deep fryer 2½kg (5lb) chips - 1 unit.

Dishwasher (cold fill) one full load - 2 units.

Extension lamp 100W 10 hours' illumination - 1 unit.

Extractor fan 24 hours' operation - 1 unit.

Floor polisher 4 hours' polishing - 1 unit.

Fluorescent strip light 40W about 20 hours' illumination - 1 unit.

Food blender 500 pints of soup - 1 unit.

Freezer (upright) per day - 1-2 units.

Fridge/freezer per day - around 2 units.

Fridge (with frozen food storage) per day - less than 1½ units.

Hair curling tongs 60 30-minute sessions - 1 unit.

Hair dryer 500W 12 10-minute sessions - 1 unit.

Hair rollers more than 20 hair do's - 1 unit.

Health lamp 100W 10 hours' use - 1 unit.

Slimline storage heaters use Economy 7. Depending on level of thermal insulation in the home, a 2kW model uses between 45 and 75 units (at less than half price) per week, during the heating season. Larger models use proportionally more.

Convector heater 2kW 30 minutes - 1 unit.

Fan heater 1kW 30 minutes - ½ unit.

Oil-filled radiator 500W 2 hours - 1 unit.

Panel heater 1.5kW 40 minutes - 1 unit.

Radiant heater 3kW 20 minutes - 1 unit.

Hot water using high performance, factory insulated 210 litre (46 gallon) Economy 7 cylinder with two side entry heaters. Hot water for a family of four per week - 67 units.

Hedge trimmer 2½ hours' use - 1 unit.

Ice cream maker 15 hours' use - 1 unit.

Instant water heater more than 3 gallons (13½ litres) of piping hot water - 1 unit.

Iron 2 hours' use - 1 unit.

Kettle 12 pints (7 litres) boiling water - 1 unit.

Knife sharpener 15,000 knives sharpened - 1 unit.

Lamp 60W 16 hours' illumination - 1 unit.

Cylinder lawnmower 3 hours' use - 1 unit.

Rotary lawnmower 1 hours' use - 1 unit.

Microwave oven 3lb (1.3kg) joint of beef - less than ½ a unit. 4 chicken pieces - ½ a unit.

Power drill 4 hours' use - 1 unit.

Shaver over 1800 shaves - 1 unit.

Shower 7kW 3-5 min shower 7 days a week - 3-4 units.

Slow cooker 8 hours' use - 1 unit.

Spin dryer 5 weeks' use - 1 unit.

Stereo 8-10 hours' listening - 1 unit.

Tape recorder more than 24 hours playing - 1 unit.

Tea maker 35 cups of tea - 1 unit.

Television (22in colour) 6-9 hours viewing - 1 unit.

Toaster 70 slices of toast - 1 unit.

Towel rail 250W 4 hours' operation - 1 unit.

Tumble dryer 9lb (4kg) cotton items dried - less than 2½units, 4½lb (2kg) synthetic items dried - less than 1½ units.

Vacuum cleaner, cylinder 1½ hours' use - 1 unit.

Vacuum cleaner, upright 2 hours' use - 1 unit.

Automatic washing machine weekly wash for 4-5 units. 9lb (4kg) cottons with pre-wash washed at 90°C - 2½ units. 4lb (1.8kg) synthetics washed at 50°C - less than 1 unit.

Waste disposer 50lb (22.5kg) of rubbish disposed - 1 unit.

Source: London Electricity Board 1991.

10. Effective homework

If you work from home be careful not to set aside rooms in your house exclusively for business purposes as this will mean you will have to pay capital gains tax on a proportion of your home when you sell it. Normally your main private residence is completely outside the capital gains tax net.

If, say, you have eight rooms and use two of them as an office, then you can claim 25% of your household running expenses such as electricity, rates and cleaning bills as a business expense. However, this concession hits back hard when you come to sell as you will be asked to pay capital gains tax on 25% of the taxable gain.

It may be that setting aside rooms for an office will be worthwhile as you will see immediate benefits in terms of the business tax liability. The capital gains tax bill is a distant threat which is softened considerably by the new indexation rules which mean you don't pay tax on gains which just reflect the rise in retail prices.

You can still claim household running expenses against your business if you use your home for work without using rooms for work and nothing but work. The rooms where you work will then still be classed as a dining room or spare bedroom and you will not have to pay capital gains tax when you come to sell.

11. Managing the bills

Do not be too enthusiastic about paying bills. Time is money. Why be a swift payer if there is no incentive? Some traders – but none of the utilities – now offer a nominal discount for prompt payment and then it makes sense to pay swiftly. Local authorities will allow you to split your annual rates bill into ten and pay the bills monthly with a two month holiday before starting again. There is no charge for delaying the payments so why pay the whole year's bill at once?

If you need to save for a hefty electricity or telephone bill do not use the 'stamps' system. If only means that 'they' get your money in advance. It would be much better to open a building society account with no withdrawal restrictions and earn interest while you are saving up to pay those nasty bills.

If you have several bills to pay take all the giros to the bank and pay them all with one cheque. This will cut down on bank charges, if you pay them, and save spending money on stamps.

12. Gardening tips

Planning ahead in the garden can save pounds. It is much cheaper to compost your own garden waste than buy expensive fertilisers. If you propagate plants from seed, even if the success rate is far from 100%, it will cost less than buying ready-grown plants. When you are building up a garden from scratch putting in immature trees and shrubs rather than buying fully grown ones will save you pounds.

Instead of buying a Christmas tree that has been sawn off at the roots, try to find one with an intact root-ball. Then you can plant it in the garden and have an extra plant. If you want to dig it up again the following Christmas to bring inside, plant it with its pot.

If you need to borrow money for a grand landscaping project, building a shed, or laying paths or a driveway, remember that the loan will be eligible for mortgage interest tax relief if you are within the £30,000 limit.

13. Built to last

If you buy modern off-the-peg furniture then it loses almost all its value the moment you take it home, but if you choose antiques you should be able to sell the pieces for as much as you paid for them, if not more. Modern furniture loses 85% to 90% of its value instantly, reproduction furniture drops 70% but antiques hardly dip at all before they start climbing.

You can buy a Georgian drop-leaf dining table in an auction for around £150 or £200. A Venetian five light chandelier will cost around £100, much cheaper than the nearest department store equivalent. Look out for the antiques of tommorow. 1960's furniture is beginning to come into vogue. You can find Sixties teak dining suites for around £100. "People thought art deco was a flash in the pan, but it has lasted," said an auction house valuer. "Who knows what will happen to the Sixties stuff." Fine Edwardian furniture has shown remarkable appreciation. A bookcase that sold for £150 four or five years ago would now be worth £500 or £600.

Check department store prices before you set off for the auction rooms and pick a sale that suits your pocket. Phillips in London, for instance, have three separate auction rooms at different levels. At the cheaper end you can usually find a few £10 lots of curios from a house clearance that no one else appreciated at the time.

14. Kitchen cuts

In the kitchen you can save money by turning your back on convenience foods. Instead of frozen, packet or tinned food, stick to fresh seasonal foods. You do not have to turn vegetarian to cut the food bill. There are plenty of cuts which take time to prepare or cook but which are much cheaper than the popular easy cuts. You can always invent a dog for the sake of your pride when asking the butcher for odd bones for soups or stews.

Find friends who will join in bulk buying foodstuffs that keep, such as rice or flour. Save fuel by stuffing the freezer with newspapers if it is not full. Always use the right sized pot for your burners and do not over fill the kettle.

Go shopping for fresh food in street markets and try supermarkets just before closing time when prices are marked down. In the last half hour of trading on Saturday afternoons supermarkets are a particularly good hunting ground – of course you could end up without any bread at all doing this! – and do not forget the basket for damaged packets and dented tins which are always sold off cheaply.

15. Decorating hints

It is not cheating to get the right effect by using your ingenuity when decorating your home. Kitchen units can cost a fortune, but you can use unpainted shuttering ply and deep mouldings to get a really luxurious country kitchen look. Putting beading or moulding on plain doors or around the edges of shelves makes ordinary D-I-Y carpentry look more professional. Standard doors can form the basis of a kitchen – cut them in half for instant cupboard doors.

You do not have to use pricey curtain material for curtains. Household linen suppliers such as Limericks of Southend (call 0702 343486 for a catalogue) are a wonderful source of cheap alternatives. Try unbleached cotton sheeting at £1.15 a metre for the 40″ wide or £3.15 a metre for the 93″ wide for lavishly draped curtains.

You can buy sheeting material of all types, candlewick, and material for tablecloths, dusters or tea towels by the metre. Not only can you save a few pennies by making things yourself but you can get the size and shape you want rather than the standard offer.

16. Enjoying your freebies

Paying rates and taxes is painful, but it is infinitely worse if you do not take advantage of the free services you have already paid for.

Why buy books when you can borrow them from the local library? Most will order books at your request and reserve popular ones for you if you cannot ever find them on the shelves. Libraries also supply records and tapes and some even lend paintings to hang on your walls.

If you are really saving hard you could also use the library for reading your daily newspaper and weekly magazines. The library is also used quite often as a venue for children's free entertainments such as puppet shows and Easter bonnet competitions.

The museums are also a good place to take children for free entertainment. Some, such as the Museum of Childhood in London, run workshops where children can learn to make simple toys or study a section of the exhibits. The National

Gallery usually provides children with a free quiz to lure them round the paintings each school holiday.

17. Heat treatment

Heating up a whole house is so costly that it makes sense to try to target heat more accurately. An electric blanket can make a slightly chilly bedroom quite bearable. You can even buy electric over-blankets or duvets which can be kept on all night for 2p per person.

Slow cookers which are plugged into the mains in the morning and cook a stew or casserole gradually during the day so working couples can come home to a ready hot meal do not waste fuel heating up a vast oven with just one pot in it.

You can even buy heaters for wellington boots to make going out in winter less of an ordeal. But for those at home, particularly the elderly, try electrically heated pads to warm cold knees or feet.

After you have had a hot bath do not throw that expensively heated water down the plug-hole to warm the sewers. Leave the plug in until the bath has gone cold and let the warmth penetrate the house even if it does get a bit steamy.

18. Cloth kit

Abandon fancy tablecloths that have to be washed after every meal and invest in a roll of cheap lining paper – the stuff that is pasted onto bare plaster walls before they are painted.

For special occasions you can draw appropriate decorations such as a birthday cake, Easter chicks or holly straight onto the 'cloth'. For formal dinner parties you can organise the seating arrangements by writing the guest's names at their places.

The paper can also be used instead of gift wrapping paper. Stick glitter or sequins on it or paint vivid squiggles to jazz it up. Children can use it as a ready supply of drawing paper, which can be torn off in huge strips when required for communal collages and the like. For the kids you should be able to find a source of free computer print-out paper that has been thrown out by a business.

19. Home principles

If you have a second home you should think carefully about how much profit you stand to make when the properties are sold. You can choose which property you call your principal private residence. Whichever one you nominate can be sold entirely free of capital gains tax, while the other one will bear the full brunt. You will have to choose at the time of purchasing your second home – not later.

It makes sense to nominate the property with the most gain as your main home. You can write to the Inland Revenue up to two years after you want the ruling to apply. If you say nothing the Revenue will work out where you spend most of your time and deem that property your main home.

There is nothing shady about changing your mind. If circumstances change and your official second home looks as if it would make you handsome gains, and you are contemplating realising the gain, then you can swop.

20. Mortgage difficulties

If you are having problems paying your mortgage the worst possible thing you can do is ignore the situation and think it will get better. True, interest rates could well come down later in the year but if you are starting to experience difficulties now the quicker you nip the problem in the bud the better the chance you have of keeping your home.

Most people faced with rising mortgage payments simply feel helpless. The key thing to remember is that you do have options and if you act straight away you will have a larger number of options and can choose the best one suited to your individual circumstances. There are various ways you can trim your monthly mortgage paments which you can discuss with your lender, be it bank or building society. Remember you are both in this together. The lender does not want to have to repossess your home and try and sell it in a depressed market. You, of course, don't want to lose the roof over your head. So here's some options:

● Cut the monthly mortgage payments by extending the life of the loan. This may be suitable if you have a repayment loan and if it has ten to fifteen years left. It's probably not an option open to those with mortgages already being repaid over twenty-five years.

● Cut the monthly mortgage payments by having a capital repayment holiday. Again this option applies to those with repayment mortgages who each month are paying a combination of interest and capital. If they just pay interest then their monthly payment is reduced.

● Ask for breathing space. If you go to your lender armed with all the facts and figures you may well be able to thrash out a mutually satisfactory agreement. This may involve a payment pause, delaying part of the interest rate so you are paying the equivalent of a lower rate than those currently being charged or even, sell your home to lender and pay rent instead.

CHAPTER SEVEN:
MOVING ON

Few of us are going to stay in the same home for the rest of our lives. Families get bigger as children are born and smaller as they grow up and leave home. Careers often require us to move from one place to another, while changing economic circumstances may mean that we want to spend more or sometimes less on where we live. You might just get bored with where you are living. You may want to be nearer family or friends or move to a more pleasant part of the country.

For whatever reason the chances are that we are all going to be moving, on average, once every five years or so. Most of us are going to be in the position of buying another home at the same time as we are selling the present one. In a few cases this will not be so, for example, if you are a first-time buyer or an elderly home owner moving into residential care.

Matter of timing

For most of us the problem is going to be sorting out the timing. Do we find another place to move to first? Or do we make sure that we have a buyer before looking around? How can we make sure that we can sell our present property and buy another at the same time without making ourselves homeless or having to borrow money to buy the new place while still paying out on our existing mortgage?

There are no satisfactory solutions to these questions. Some deals go through very smoothly with buyers and sellers fitting in with each others' plans. Other transactions take a long time, especially where a chain of several buyers and sellers is involved. In those cases everyone in the chain has to wait until the slowest has made their arrangements and then everyone moves at more or less the same pace. In some cases the deals do not go through for one reason or another and every seller has to be prepared to take the risk that the sale of their home will be subject to delay or worse still a complete breakdown in negotiations.

Having decided to sell and prepared yourself for the worst, one of the first things you will have to sort out is where you are going to live. There is little point in putting your home on the market and involving everyone in all the fuss of selling, if you find that you have nowhere to go and are forced to back out of the sale.

It seems a silly point but a surprising number of people go along with a sale only to find that they have not found their dream home or that their own purchase has fallen through leaving them with little option but to delay the sale of their home or even to take the property off the market. This may be unavoidable where you are yourself being let down. However, the buyers of your property will have spent money on surveys and legal advice and they are not going to be very pleased if you back out at the last minute.

In some cases there may be no option but to sell without having found alternative accommodation. This might give you extra flexibility if you move in with friends or into rented accommodation as a temporary measure. But this is a very disruptive process and will involve you in two moves. If you are staying with friends, remember that it could take six months or more to buy a new place and even the best friendships can wear a bit thin in that time.

In many areas of the country your money will be best left in the property where it will increase in value faster than if you put the money in a bank or a building society account. Conversely, there are some areas in the country where house prices are static and your money might be better off in a savings account. It all depends on what's happening to property prices and what level of return you could earn on cash deposited in a bank or building society.

Preparing your property

Once you have decided to put your property on the market make sure that it looks as presentable as possible. Small decorating and repair jobs can make an enormous difference to the impression potential buyers get of your home when they look round. If it is neat and tidy they are more likely to buy and to pay more. Don't ignore the front, and back, garden too.

Do not, however, go to the extent of putting in major improvements or modifications in order to sell your property. While some improvements will increase its value, central heating for example, most will not justify the cost if you are intending to move immediately. Remember too that one man's home improvement is another's act of vandalism. What you regard as a major improvement might be the first thing that the new owner rips out.

However, there are some major repairs which will prove cost effective. A bad damp problem, for example, or evidence of dry rot, can knock the price of a property down out of all proportion to the cost of putting the defects right. In that case you may be advised to get the work done yourself before selling.

When to sell

There are really no hard and fast rules about when is the best time to sell your home. Obviously personal circumstances will play a big role here. In general, though, you are likely to find it difficult in a time of falling house prices or when mortgage finance is very costly or in short supply. You will have some idea of what your house is worth, but do not be surprised if potential buyers do not have the same figure in mind. You may have to lower your sights to secure a quick sale. If prices are rising then you may find it pays to sit tight for the time being. Traditionally the main home buying season is said to be in the spring but building societies' figures show that this is less of a peak than it used to be.

Moving on checklist

Make sure you have all the facts at your fingertips that potential buyers are likely to need. Much of this information you will be required to provide when the buyer's solicitor sends a standard form 'enquiries before contract' to your solicitor to fill in. But it is as well to be prepared in advance. You should have details of:

- Rates bills
- Heating bills and other outgoings on the property
- Service charges, if any
- Ground rent, if any
- NHBC guarantee (if any)
- Timber treatment and damp proof guarantees
- Any facilities you share with other householders (e.g. a driveway)
- Any disputes you have had with neighbours over the previous three years

● Fixtures and fittings. Make sure you are clear about what counts as a fitting, what you wish to include in the price of the house and what will be an extra.

There are three ways that you can go about finding a buyer for your home. You can go through an estate agent, a property shop or try and sell it yourself.

Estate agent

Most people still use estate agents when they are selling their property – often the agent who sold them the house originally. In many areas, there is really no alternative to using the local estate agent, unless you are going to sell your house yourself.

It should not be too difficult finding an estate agent to sell your property for you. A local agent will probably be the best choice. Anyone looking for the type of property you are trying to sell will usually go to the local estate agents to see what they have on offer.

If you have a house to sell then the chances are you probably know the local estate agents. If in any doubt, you can easily find them in the local Yellow pages, by buying the local newspaper or checking the agents' boards outside properties in your area.

While you do not need to employ an estate agent to sell your home for you, the arguments in favour of doing so go like this. They will take away the worry of selling your house (unlikely), they will advertise the property in the local press (sometimes), they will put your property on their books (always) and will offer it to people who are on their lists as looking for this type of property in a particular location and price range (always).

Estate agents also argue that they get the best price for your property because they know the local market and can therefore price your property accordingly and that they have a list of potential buyers who are poised to pull out their cheque books. Estate agents are on commission, which means that it is in their interest that you get the best price.

Many of these claims can be taken with a pinch of salt. An estate agent is as good or as bad as the people it employs. Some offer a good service, reasonably priced for the effort and expertise involved. Some are just in it for the money and aim to get it by doing as little as they can. Ask around friends and neighbours to see if you can get a consensus of opinion about the local agents. You may be surprised to find that the flashy new office with the potted palms and micro-computers has a bad reputation with people who have used it, while an older, more fuddy-duddy, firm has a reputation for fairness and honesty. Or, it might be the other way round.

Good agents will come round when they say they are going to come – not an hour later. They will take copious notes on the property and give you a valuation. Many agents boast about their so-called 'free' valuation service. This service is their main way of getting business and the costs are covered in sales commission.

A good agent will set a fair price for your property, but don't be afraid to use your own judgement. You should get a good idea of the value of your home by looking at similar properties on the market in your neighbourhood. You will find these in estate agents' windows and the local newspaper. Beware of estate agents who just ask you what you think your property is worth. They are supposed to be offering a professional service, not asking you to do their job for them.

It is advisable to get several agents around to give you a valuation. This will give you a better idea of the sort of price your property can command. However, it does not automatically follow that you should instruct the agent who gives you the highest valuation. The art of valuing is in setting the highest price at which the property will be sold within a reasonable period of time.

Owners often have an over optimistic idea of the value of their house. However, in some cases you may have a much better idea of the value of local property than the agent. After all it is your house and your money that is at stake.

Having valued the house the agent should then provide particulars and take photographs of the property to give to prospective buyers. This involves measuring the rooms and identifying any interesting or attractive features of the property as well as any improvements or additions that will be selling points. These might include a new roof, central heating, double glazing, conservatory, a well-stocked garden and so on.

A good agent may advise on repairs that are necessary

before the property is put on the market. Some improvements will be justified by bringing a better price for the property than would otherwise be obtained. Other improvements, although necessary, might cost more than they are worth when the house is eventually sold.

Other duties of the estate agent are to co-ordinate visits by potential buyers. A good agent will show prospective buyers around personally. However, in areas of fast moving property or during a house buying boom, such niceties often get dispensed with, and you the seller are obliged to do the agent's job for him.

A good agent should also advise on, and co-ordinate, offers made by prospective buyers for the house and keep track of all the interested parties and what they are prepared to pay.

The agent should also judge how serious the potential buyers are and whether they have the ability to raise the money for the purchase. There is no point in you accepting an offer from a potential buyer who subsequently discovers that they cannot afford your house. A good agent will also help you in any subsequent negotiations, for example, after the potential buyers have had their own survey report carried out. Often a survey report will uncover problems with the property, which may affect the price the buyer is willing to pay.

Estate agents' charges

Estate agents charge on average around 2% plus VAT of the selling price for their services. However this commission rate varies up and down the country, to a high of 3% in some of the pricier areas of London down to 1% in some parts of Scotland and the North of England.

Commission rates are usually lower by about ½% if the agent is given sole agency. This is not advisable unless you have an unusual or high priced property which would not fit on many agents' books. It means that he or she is the only estate agent acting for you. In some parts of the country agents still offer lower commission rates for so-called 'sole selling rights'. This practice, now thankfully dying out, means that the agent can charge you the commission even if you sell the house yourself. You should avoid giving an agent sole selling rights at all costs.

Make sure at the outset you know what the agent is going to charge. In the North it is common for agents to charge around 1½% plus the cost of advertising. Other agents will include advertising in their basic fee. Remember too that fees are negotiable. There is no law that says an agent must get 2%. You may be able to haggle over the fee.

Even at 2% the cost of selling a house seems very high. On an average sale of around £40,000 this means the agent will charge £800. In London, where an average sale price could be around £60,000 and many quite ordinary houses change hands for over £80,000, sellers are finding themselves increasingly reluctant to pay the £1,200 to £1,600 estate agency fees that are charged on such sales.

Property shop

The property shop works in much the same way as an estate agent but instead of the shop taking a commission based on the sale price of the house, they charge a flat fee, usually up-front, ranging between £100 and £150. The advantages are that you know in advance what you are going to pay and it is obviously a lot cheaper than most estate agents. The disadvantage is that you pay the money whether or not the house is sold through the property shop. In general, the shop will keep your property on their books indefinitely.

The service provided by property shops varies and there have been some well publicised failures in this new way of selling homes, notably Woolworth's decision to get rid of its in-store property shops. However, there are reputable property shops around who offer a reasonable service for a reasonable price.

Arguments against the property shop idea, which incidentally usually come from estate agents, are that they do not try to get the best price for their client because they are on a fixed fee. There is some truth in this, but you will have to decide for yourself whether the property shop is the best route for you. The property shops defend themselves by pointing out that they usually try and sell the house at the price set by the seller. This is a price which usually compares with the price of similar properties in the area being handled by estate agents.

They also point out that because they are charging a flat fee of perhaps £100 sale or no sale, the seller of the house has greater flexibility to drop the price without taking an overall loss. For example, if the property is for sale at £50,000, then an estate agent charging 2% would take £1,000 if he or she sold the property at that price. By selling through the property shop the seller could drop that price by up to £900 and still come out after the house has been sold with £49,000 – the same as if it had been sold through the estate agent at the higher original asking price.

Whether you accept that argument or not will probably depend on your own past experience with estate agents. You might feel that they justify their 2% by getting a higher price for your home and helping with the negotiations.

DIY route

There are obvious ways you can go about this. You can put a 'for sale' sign in the window, try a notice in the local newsagent's window or advertise in the local or national newspapers. The local newspaper is probably going to be the most cost-effective way of getting your message across. Estate agents advertise heavily in local papers, and these usually include special space for private sellers to put details of their house in the paper. A small advertisement will cost you perhaps £10 to £15. However, you may have to keep advertising for several weeks until you get someone interested.

The national newspapers are increasingly interested in cashing in on the house selling act, especially the Sunday newspapers. The costs of advertising here are more than double for the local newspaper and it is questionable whether readers of the paper in Perth are going to be interested in you selling your house in Penzance – but you never know.

Sundays and nationals often do special deals under which they will carry the same ad for several weeks at a reduced rate. It is worth enquiring what offers the paper is making.

It is a fact of life that people who are looking for a house to buy in the main still go to estate agents. So far estate agents have been relatively immune from competition. This may change in the future as big financial institutions, such as banks, building societies and insurance companies, buy their way into the estate agency market.

In the interim, though, you may find that it takes longer to sell your house yourself than through an established agent. If you are not in a rush to sell, then you can afford to adopt a more leisurely timetable. Remember too that putting your house in the hands of an established agent does not prevent you from making moves to sell it yourself. Check, however, that you have not agreed to 'sole selling rights' with an agent you have instructed. This means that even if you sell the house yourself, you would still be obliged to pay the estate agent.

A date to view

Once you start getting some interest in the property you may have to handle most of the selling yourself. Estate agents used to show potential buyers around themselves as part of the service they offered. In many parts of the country they still do. However, where property is moving fast it is a custom that is dying out and you may find that you will have to do the honours. Honesty is generally the best policy when dealing with enquiries from potential buyers looking around your property. However, there is no need to go overboard and in fact the law discourages you from offering too much information about your property.

In general, the principle of 'Caveat Emptor' prevails, which means 'let the buyer beware'. It is the buyer's responsibility to check that the property is up to scratch. You can put yourself in a potentially difficult situation by giving too much information. If this subsequently proves to be wrong, the buyer could have grounds for ending the contract and claiming damages. At the same time, there is no point in trying to hide things that are patently wrong with the property: for example, if the back extension is riddled with damp. You should take such things into account when you put a price on your home but be prepared to re-negotiate the price once the buyer's surveyor has been around.

The offer

When a potential buyer puts in an offer for your property you should have a fair idea of whether they can in fact afford to pay for it. When they come round to view ask them about their circumstances.

Do they have a house to sell? How far have they got with it? If they are not selling a house do they have mortgage finance agreed? Obviously there is a limit to the amount of information that you can reasonably ask a potential buyer, but you do have the right to know how serious are their intentions. Some people after all make a pastime out of looking around people's homes on the pretext that they are buying without having any real intention of doing so at all. If they are living in rented accommodation or do not have property to sell this puts them in a stronger position as buyers. They can move fast if they want to.

Most buyers in England and Wales will try an offer below your asking price in the first instance. It is after all better to start low when offering money and then raise your price, depending on how much you want the house. As the seller, you should have a clear idea of the price you want for your home.

If you are getting a lot of interest and offers then the probability is that you have priced it too low. Conversely if there is little interest and you get an offer for below the sale price then you will have to decide how quickly you want to sell.

How you go about handling a number of potential buyers and dealing with their offers on the property is largely a matter of personal morality. If you agree to sell to A for £39,000 and B comes along a couple of weeks later and offers £40,000 the choice of action in England and Wales is up to you.

Offers are usually subject to survey and contract. The buyer reserves the right to re-negotiate the price once a survey has been carried out on the property. The seller is not legally bound by an agreed price until exchange of contracts. The important exception to this is Scotland where offers are legally binding.

If the second offer you receive is substantially higher than the first, then the least you can do is to go back to the first person and ask them whether they can match the new offer. Be prepared for the fact that they will not be too pleased about this. After all they may have paid for survey and legal fees as well as agreeing to sell their own property on the basis of buying yours at the stated price.

In England and Wales until contracts have been exchanged there are no obligations on you the seller at all apart from the moral code which dictates that you should behave in a reasonable and honorable fashion. Provided you bide your time and wait until all of the interested parties have put in their offers you should not run into too many difficulties. If you suspect that someone is interested and another buyer is pressing you for a decision you could always ring them up and prompt them into either making an offer or dropping out of the buying.

Major problems can arise over fixtures and fittings which are a grey area in terms of the law. If you use an estate agent they will detail in the particulars of sale what is included in the sale price. Fixtures do not generally include such things as curtain rails, light bulbs or light shades although ceiling roses, for example, are and will generally be included in the sale price.

Carpets and curtains are not usually regarded as fixtures and will not be included in the sale price. If you decide to leave the carpets and curtains in the house you are selling you can put a price on them – say £1,000 or whatever you think the buyer will pay. Remember that the cost of putting in carpets and curtains is no real guide to the price you will get for them. They do not have a good second hand value. If you can use them in your new home all well and good. You may find that the buyers do not like your choice of carpets or curtains and will not want to buy them anyway.

In some instances where the property is valued at just over £30,000 it may be possible to set the price at £29,000 plus the difference for fixtures and fittings. This has the effect of reducing the price to below the £30,000 level at which stamp duty is payable on the sale.

The surveyor's visit

Once you have accepted an offer, the buyer will normally want to send a surveyor round to look at the property and will reserve the right to re-negotiate the price depending on the results of his or her report. Unless you are dealing with a cash buyer, it is virtually certain that some kind of valuation or survey will be made on the property. The least that you can expect is for the building society or the mortgage lender to send someone around to value the property.

The buyer might want a fuller survey conducted, however, which can take anything up to half a day depending on the extent of the survey. While this may be an inconvenience remember that the buyer is preparing to fork out a very large sum of money and has every right to make sure of the property's condition. Once the survey has been completed and a valuation placed on the property, the buyer might decide not to go ahead or try to re-negotiate the price. This is par for the course because in England and Wales until contracts have been signed and exchanged neither party is legally obliged to complete the deal. However, most people don't pay survey fees for fun, so unless your home is badly in need of repairs it is unlikely the buyer will disappear completely from sight at this stage.

They may simply re-open negotiations. Depending on how much of a reduction they want, you may decide either to put the property back on the market or to re-negotiate the price. If you feel there is a strong demand for the property at the original price, or prices are rising fast, then look for another buyer. If you want to sell quickly, perhaps because you have another purchase going through, it may be better to negotiate. Try splitting the difference between the price you wish to sell at and the new price offered.

Until now for those of you living in England and Wales there has been no actual need to contact your solicitor. However, it is as well to put your solicitor in the picture as soon as possible, perhaps when you put the property on the market. They won't actually do anything, but they will at least be aware that you are in the process of selling. You may be doing your own conveyancing in which case you will not need to contact a solicitor at all. The conveyancing involved when you sell is much simpler than when you buy. However, as most people will probably be both buyer and seller at the same time and up to their necks in the hassles involved with co-ordinating two property transactions, a solicitor can mean the difference between relative sanity and chaos.

Stages involved in selling

1. Get the house valued. You can either do this yourself or get a local estate agent to value it. It is often better to get several opinions before making a final decision.
2. Instruct an estate agent, property shop or start advertising the property yourself. If you are using an agent decide whether you are giving him or her 'sole agency' which will usually be cheaper or whether you are putting the property with several agents. Avoid any agent who demands 'sole selling rights', even if he is charging a lower commission.
3. Negotiate the fee. Estate agents must agree charges when you instruct them to sell for you. You can argue about the price but agents usually work on a straight percentage commission. Property shops usually charge a flat fee – but remember you pay the money whether the property is sold or not.
4. Decide what is included in the sale price and what you are going to charge for extras. Fixtures are usually included in the overall price, while carpets and curtains are negotiated separately.
5. Keep the house clean and tidy for potential buyers to look around. Do not get involved in major repairs and improvements which will not increase the selling price.
6. Those homeowners in England and Wales should agree a price with a buyer subject to contract. Make sure that you have got all the offers in that you are likely to get. Don't panic and sell to the first buyer who makes an offer. Negotiate a separate price for carpets and curtains and other items not included in the sale price. In Scotland, an offer is legally binding and once you accept it, you cannot change your mind without suffering financial consequences.

7. Be prepared to re-negotiate the price once the buyer has had a valuation and/or survey on the property.
8. Tell your solicitor, who can then start to draw up a contract.
9. You will receive a questionnaire of 'preliminary' enquiries from the buyer's solicitors which you must complete and return.
10. Do not sign and send off your copy of the contract until you are sure that your own house purchase or other accommodation arrangements are being sorted out. There is no point in making yourself homeless for the sake of clinching a sale.

Bridging loans

While you should try as far as possible to make sure that your property purchase coincides with the sale of your existing property this may not be possible. Very often you may find that your buyer has to drop out at a late stage or is delayed, perhaps because their buyer in turn cannot complete on time. Such 'chains' of house buyers and sellers can severely inhibit the speed of your move, slowing it down to the rate of the slowest member.

In order to break the chain you need to complete the purchase of your new property before you have sold your old one. The usual way of doing this is to take out a bridging loan from your bank. There are two main situations where you may require bridging finance. First, to cover the 10% deposit on exchange of contracts. Second, to cover the entire purchase price at completion. However since the new legislation covering building societies came into force in 1987 they are free to arrange unsecured loans and can offer to lend you money for the deposit as well as the eventual mortgage.

If we assume you are selling a £40,000 property and are buying a £60,000 property then even if you synchronise transactions your buyer will only pay you a deposit of £4,000 while you require £6,000 on exchange of contracts to pay the owner of the house you plan to buy.

If you do not manage to synchronise your exchange of contracts you may have to 'bridge' the entire 10% of the purchase price, that is £6,000. You can try asking the seller to accept a deposit of less than 10%, but they in turn probably need the money to finance their own purchase. The bank will usually consider lending you the money provided that contracts are exchanged and a date set for completion. This is what's called a closed bridge. The manager may consider an open bridge where no final date is set for completion provided you can afford the repayments but they will be less keen. Most banks will require an undertaking from your solicitor that he or she will forward the bank the money from the sale of your house.

The other situation where you may need a bridging loan is where you need to complete on your purchase, before you have sold your own house. Again the bank will normally only be willing to do this if you have already exchanged contracts for the sale of your house, or failing that if you provide sufficient security, perhaps by lodging the deeds of both your existing and new homes with them or leaving some investments in their care.

Make sure that you get a certificate from the bank indicating that the loan is for a bridge so that you can claim tax relief in the same way as on your mortgage. An ordinary overdraft or personal loan from the bank is not normally eligible for tax relief. Only use bridging finance as a last resort. It is expensive and you are likely to be charged at least 3% or 4% over the bank's base rate as well as an arrangement fee of between £50 and £100.

Breaking the housing chain

There are other schemes available which aim to break the housebuying chain. These usually involve a third party, such as an estate agent or a housebuilder, if you are buying a new house, buying your house from you rather in the same way a car dealer will take your old car when you buy a new one in part exchange. However, as with used car dealers, such middle-men will not buy your home unless they think they can make a quick profit. Where estate agents offer to buy your house, they will usually suggest a price which is below the market price of your house. It may be 5% or 10% less. This is so they can cover their transaction costs and finance keeping the property on their books until they find a buyer.

Be sure you understand the deal before agreeing to it or you may find yourself accepting a price for your house which is way below what it is worth. Similarly with new housebuilders, who are offering 'part exchange' deals if you buy a new house from them. Make sure you obtain a firm figure from them which they are prepared to pay for your house. You can then weigh up whether it is a good deal or whether you should wait until a genuine buyer comes along.

The move

Depending on how many possessions you have, you might just hire a van and get a few friends to help you with the move. If you have a family or are moving for the second or third time, the chances are that you might need to employ the services of a 'professional' removal firm. If you use a professional company check that they belong to a trade body like the British Association of Removers which has a code of conduct for its members. Also check what insurance arrangements you will need for the move. The removers may provide you with some protection, but for valuable items or objects requiring specialist removal skills you may have to buy your own insurance. If you already have insurance cover ask the company whether they will cover you for the move. You may find that they will automatically do this, but it is as well to check in advance. At the same time remember to transfer your insurance cover to the new address.

Disputes with removal firms most often arise over breakages. So make sure that the price they are quoting you for the job includes insurance.

The cost of actual moving depends on how much you have, how far you are moving, and how long it takes to move. For an average move though you can reckon on not getting any change from £200. You can save money by using a small local firm, but if anything goes wrong that small saving may prove costly. Far better to pay a bit more to hire the services of a member of the British Association of Removers. You can contact them on 071-837 3088 at 279 Grays Inn Road, London WC1, and they will give you a list of local firms.

GLOSSARY

ABI
Association of British Insurers. The main trade association for insurance companies in the United Kingdom. Nearly all companies belong to it. The ABI was formed in 1985 following the merger of several smaller trade associations. It runs a public enquiries service for consumers who have queries on a range of insurance matters.

Accidental Damage Cover
Usually bought as an extra on a household insurance policy for an additional payment. Many household insurance policies are available with or without this option. An example of accidental damage would be drilling through a concealed water pipe while fixing a kitchen unit to the wall. Accidental damage cover pays the repair bill, subject of course to any reference in the small print that you have to pay the first portion of a claim.

Advance
Another term for a loan.

All Risks
A description often used for very wide cover under a household or travel insurance policy. It does not mean literally what it says, so still check the small print for exclusions. However, an all-risk household policy will cover a wide range of accidents inside or outside the home.

Average
The reduction of a claim payment because of under insurance. If the contents of a house are insured for less than their true value then any claim will be reduced in proportion to the underinsurance. So, for example, if you are underinsured by 30% and you claim £90, you will be paid £60.

Bridging Loan
A short term loan to tide over a purchaser who is waiting to receive cash from the sale of a property. Provided the loan is to help the buyer purchase his or her main residence, which

in turn is occupied within twelve months, tax relief is available on the interest payments of the bridging loan.

Capital Gains Tax
Individuals who make a profit from selling a capital asset such as shares, jewellery or a second home must pay tax on any gains over and above the standard allowance. For the year 1990-91 this allowance is £5,000. So, by careful timing of the sale of crucial items, most people should be able to avoid a capital gains tax bill.

Collateral
Security that a bank may seek before agreeing to lend you money. Typical collateral would include stocks and shares, a life policy or a charge over your house.

Commission
Fee paid by a financial institution to a third party who concludes a sale of their products to a member of the public. It is usually calculated as a percentage of the sum invested, borrowed or paid by the customer.

Completion
A formal meeting between solicitors for the purchaser and seller of the property to hand over the purchase money and conclude the last formalities.

Declinature
A rejection by an insurance company of a proposal for insurance. If you have been turned down before you must usually tell the company on any subsequent proposal form you fill out. If you don't, you may find out that when you come to claim, the company refuses to pay out on the grounds it was not fully informed of all the material circumstances when it set the fee for the policy.

Decreasing Term Assurance
The sum assured reduces each year or month by a stated amount reaching nil at the end of the term. It is usually used to cover a reducing debt such as a mortgage, in which case it is called a mortgage protection plan.

Disclosure
The legal burden on someone applying for insurance cover to disclose every relevant fact, even if there is not a question specifically asked on the proposal form. Consumer groups have been lobbying unsuccessfully to reduce this burden on customers.

Domicile
This is a legal term. Broadly speaking it applies to the country where you have a permanent home. It is distinct from residence or nationality. It is possible to be a residence in more than one country, but you can only be domiciled in one place at any given time. Normally people adopt the domicile of their father. Before 1974 married women shared the domicile of their husbands and kept this even if widowed or divorced. Since January 1, 1974 the rules governing the domicile of married women are exactly the same as for everybody else.

Endowment Assurance
This is a form of life assurance where the sum assured is payable either when the policy matures or on a policyholder's death, if earlier. As there is a guarantee of a payout, endowment assurance can be used as security for a long term loan such as a mortgage.

Endowment Mortgage
Here the home loan is linked to an endowment plan, a life assurance savings product. The borrower's monthly instalments covers the interest on the home loan and a monthly premium to an insurance company. At the end of the term of the loan the sum accumulated in the endowment policy is used to repay the debt and any surplus is kept by the borrower. In the event of the borrower's death the loan is repaid in full under this method. There are three types of endowment mortgage, non-profit, with-profits and low cost. Basically the higher the premium invested in the insurance plan the greater the potential for the borrower to be left with a lump sum after the mortgage has been repaid.

Estate Agent
The agent is hired by the owner of a house, known as the vendor, to arrange for potential purchasers to view the house and negotiate the price on behalf of the seller. In return for these services he or she charges a fee, usually expressed as a percentage of the selling price, which is paid by the vendor.

Excess
An agreed amount of each insurance claim that policyholders have to pay themselves. This can range from £10 to £200, depending on the policy and the company. You can often reduce the cost of your insurance policy by volunteering to pay a higher excess than normal.

Exchange Contracts
The technical term for completing a transaction, such as a house purchase. This occurs when all searches and enquiries have been completed. The purchase usually becomes irrevocable and is binding on both parties when contracts are exchanged.

Exclusions
The risks that an insurance policy does not cover. If in any doubt, ask in writing and keep the reply for future use.

First Loss
A policy which covers only the first part of a loss on some specialist insurance, where the insurance company is not prepared to take on an open-ended commitment.

Ground Rent
Payment to landlord under the lease. This is usually due every year at a preset sum.

Home Improvement Grants
A grant given by your local council to cover part of the cost of certain improvements to your home. There are four separate kinds of grant. Improvement grants for major improvements, associated repairs and conversions. Intermediate grants for putting in missing standard amenities eg inside toilet, bath, sink, hot and cold water. Repair grants for pre-1919 houses which

need substantial and structural repairs. Special grants for putting in standard amenities and means of escape from fire in houses in multiple occupation. Intermediate grants are mandatory and your local council cannot refuse to give you this money if you qualify. The other grants are normally discretionary.

Home Income Plans
These enable retired home owners to generate an income for life by borrowing against the value of their house. The loan is repaid by the borrower's estate when they die.

Home Reversion Plan
These are a way of raising capital on a home that the owner still wants to live in. The home owner sells a reversionary interest in his or her house to the promoter of the scheme but retains a legal right to live rent free in the house for rest of his or her life and if applicable, the rest of the spouse's life.

House (or Home) Contents Insurance
This covers possessions, fixtures and fittings. There are two main types of home contents insurance: indemnity terms and new-for-old. Indemnity means you receive a sum equal to the original value minus wear and tear, whereas with new-for-old you get a sum sufficient to replace the article at today's prices. Some items may additionally be insured on an all-risks basis, which means they are covered outside the house as well.

Household Insurance
Combined policy covering both buildings and home contents insurance.

Housing Benefit
A very complicated system introduced in 1983 which gives help with housing costs in the form of rent and rate rebates, and rent allowances for private tenants. Those receiving supplementary benefit are automatically entitled to housing benefit. Others should apply to their local authority.

Indemnity terms
A type of home contents insurance policy that pays only the

present value of items lost or damaged, after deducting money for wear and tear.

Index Linked Insurance
Insurance where the amount of cover automatically increases each year in line with inflation.

Inheritance Tax
This is payable on the transfer of assets at death to anyone other than your spouse if your estate is greater than the tax free band. It is also payable on gifts made during your lifetime within seven years of your death or if the transfer is not made to anyone other than an individual or an accumulation and maintenance trust.

Insurable Interest
If you have a legal or financial interest in a property or the outcome of a specific event then you can buy cover to protect your interest.

Insurance Broker
Independent insurance salesman. If he is selling life assurance he will have to be authorised by a self regulatory body set up under the Financial Services Act. If he is selling general insurance such as motor or household he will have to be registered with the Insurance Brokers Registration Council.

Joint Life
Life assurance policy on two people. There are two basic types; one that pays out on the death of the first person and one that pays out on the death of the second person.

Joint Tenancy
A property which is jointly owned by two or more people, usually husband and wife. If one dies, the other owns the whole property.

Land Registry
The register provides details of property ownership and a record of all transactions. When a piece of property changes hands this information must be registered. A fee is charged for this service based on the sale price.

Lease
A legal document designating ownership of the property to a
stated person for a fixed period of time. It details the rights
and obligations of various parties, such as who is responsible
for maintenance and repair.

Level Term Assurance
The simplest form of term assurance. The policy will pay out
an agreed fixed sum on the death of the person whose life is
covered. When the policy term finishes there is no money
returned as with some life assurance policies. This is very cheap
and excellent value.

Life Assurance
General term describing a wide range of policies that have one
thing in common - they pay out on the death of the person
insured. Some policies have a high investment content and
relatively small element of protection.

Life Assured
The person whose life is covered by an insurance policy.

Loss Adjusters
An independent insurance claims expert called in by an insurance
company to assess the value of a claim.

Loss Assessor
An independent insurance claims expert called in by a
policyholder to assess the value of the claim, especially if there
is a dispute about the sum with the insurance company.

Low Cost Whole Life Assurance
A combination of whole life assurance and decreasing term
assurance. Its main feature is a guaranteed level of cover. The
term assurance decreases as the bonuses build up in the whole
life policy and it reduces to zero as soon as the value of the
whole life policy matches the guaranteed level of cover, the
death benefit.

Low Start Policy
Usually a form of low cost endowment policy aimed at the first

time home buyer who has little to spend in the early years but expects to earn higher wages in the future. The cost of the policy is kept very low for, say, the first five years. Then there is an increase to make up for the lower payments in the policy's early years.

MIRAS
Mortgage interest relief at source. Tax relief on most loans up to £30,000 for house purchase or improvement. Under MIRAS, introduced in 1983, most borrowers pay a rate of interest net of their income tax level to the bank or building society, which will then reclaim the tax relief from the Inland Revenue.

Mortgage
Strange as it may seem building societies do not grant mortgages. Instead it is the homebuyer who gives a mortgage to the society or bank providing the loan. A mortgage is a legal charge on a property.

Mortgagee
The institution which provides the mortgage.

Mortgagor
The person who takes out a mortgage.

Mortgage Debenture
A loan secured against the asset of a property. It usually ranks ahead of both debenture holders and ordinary shareholders.

Mortgage Deed
A legal contract between a housebuyer and the lending institution financing the purchase. It includes all the relevant details about the property, its upkeep, the loan, the repayment terms of the loan and the legal rights over the property which are vested in the lender until the loan has been repaid.

Mortgage Protection Policy
Decreasing term assurance taken out in conjunction with a repayment mortgage to ensure the loan is repaid if the borrower dies. The sum assured decreases as the loan is paid off.

Mortgage Rate

The rate of interest charged on a mortgage. Most mortgages are priced on a variable basis which means the cost to the borrower moves up and down in line with rates of interest in the economy as a whole. Some societies charge a premium rate over their base mortgage rate on large loans, those linked to endowment policies, or on properties of certain types or age.

National House Building Council

The NHBC is an independent government approved body which aims to uphold building standards in this country. Since 1966 the Building Societies Association has recommended that its members only lend money on new houses constructed by housebuilders registered with the NHBC, unless the construction was supervised by an architect or qualified surveyor acting solely for the purchaser. From the housebuyer's point of view there are a number of advantages in dealing with a registered house builder. These include a fund from which money can be repaid if the builder goes bust, a guarantee to correct any defects that show up within the first two years and, between the second year and the tenth year, insurance cover against claims for major stuctural damage due to failure to comply with the council's guidelines.

New-for-Old

Home contents insurance that repays the policyholder with suffficient money to cover the current replacement cost of any item lost or damaged.

Non-Profit Endowment Mortgage

The proceeds of the endowment policy are just sufficient to repay the mortgage. The borrower does not receive a lump sum. This is usually the cheapest form of endowment policy that can be used to generate money to repay a mortgage.

Offer

In property terms, making an offer means to name a price at which you are willing to buy. In Scotland, once an offer has been made and is accepted a legally binding agreement is in force. Elsewhere in the United Kingdom, a legally binding agreement is not in place until the contracts have been formally exchanged.

On Risk
The full acceptance by an insurance company of a proposal. From the moment it is put on risk the insurance company will pay out on any genuine claims.

Pensions Mortgage
The repayment of your home can be linked to the proceeds from a pension plan, which has the added advantage of being able to grow tax free. As tax relief is available on pension contributions this can be a very attractive route but care should be taken to make sure that a sufficient sum is set aside for retirement.

Personal Insurance Arbitration Service
Set up by the insurance industry in 1981 and administered by the Institute of Arbitrators. Comparatively few companies belong to it. Its pronouncements are binding on both parties. It can make fairly limited financial awards against companies.

Policyholder's Protection Act
Established in 1975 after a series of insurance company failures. Under the Act a board administers the policies issued by any failed insurance company. In general, it guarantees policyholders 90% of any money due. The board imposes a levy on all insurance companies to raise any money it needs.

Principal
The sum borrowed. With a repayment mortgage the monthly instalments consist of both interest and repayment of principal. However, with an endowment mortgage the principal is only repaid at the end of term.

Property Insurance
Cover against a property being damaged by risks such as fire, flood, weather damage and subsidence. It is usually called buildings insurance when referring to domestic property.

Red Lining
The term used to describe certain 'no-go' credit areas where lenders would refuse automatically to give credit regardless of the individual customer's circumstances.

Redemption
The technical term for the final instalment on your mortgage. A few building societies still charge a redemption fee for those borrowers who wish to repay their mortgage early.

Reinstatement
1. A type of insurance cover for buildings where no deduction is made for wear and tear when a claim is paid.
2. The reviving of a life assurance policy after a period of non-payment of instalments. When payments stop the policy ceases to be effective. However, if the policyholder wishes to start paying again then the policy may be reinstated at the discretion of the insurance company.

Renewal
The continuation of an annual insurance policy such as a motor or household insurance policy for another period.

Renewal Notice
The notice sent to the policyholders reminding them that an insurance policy is due for renewal and more money is due.

Renewable Term Assurance
A term assurance plan that gives the consumer the option to renew at the end of its term on the same rates and without any new evidence of good health being required, provided the policyholder is below a certain age, usually 65 or 70, when the renewal option comes up.

Rent Allowance
This is the cash help available for private tenants paying high rents on low incomes. It is part of the housing benefit system and also applies to those living in mobile homes, or on a houseboat.

Rent Rebate

This may be claimed from local authority housing departments by council tenants and those who are buying their home under a shared ownership scheme. It is part of the housing benefit system and very difficult to work out who is entitled to how much.

Repayment Mortgage

With a repayment loan, a fixed sum is paid each month which covers both the interest and the debt itself. In the early years most of the monthly payment is in fact interest, where near the end of the loan's life most of the money goes towards repaying the debt itself. Traditionally the repayment or annuity method of repaying a mortgage was the most popular.

Report and Valuation

This is offered by members of the Royal Institute of Chartered Surveyors. It falls short of a full structural survey of the property but provides additional information over and above that included in a valuation.

Retention

Part of a loan which is set aside until the would-be borrower has completed certain tasks. Frequently building societies or banks withhold part of the home loan until the borrower has supplied evidence that he or she has improved the property in the way requested.

Shared Ownership Schemes

These are available through housing associations and building societies and financed by the Housing Corporation. They are designed for people who have insufficient funds to buy their home outright. Purchasers are usually first time buyers with priority going to local authority or housing association tenants and those on waiting lists. The minimum proportion you are required to buy outright will depend upon the scheme but may be as low as 25%. For further details see the leaflet Shared Ownership published by the Housing Corporation, 149 Tottenham Court Road, London W1P 0BN. Tel: 071-387 9466.

Sole Agency

When an estate agent is given the sole right to offer a property for sale over a fixed period. There is usually a discount in fees if the seller agrees to use sole agency.

Solicitors' Property Centres

These are common in Scotland but virtually unknown elsewhere in the United Kingdom. The centre keeps details of a large number of properties but unlike an estate agent will not normally arrange for the property to be visited.

Stamp Duty

A tax payable on the purchase of ordinary shares, preference shares, convertible loan stock and homes over £30,000.

Standard Indemnity Scheme Guarantee

If a building society agrees to lend you a very high proportion of the house's value, say over 75%, it normally requires additional security. This will usually consist of an agreement from an insurance company that it will guarantee the additional percentage. The borrower will be asked to pay a one-off premium to cover this insurance. Rates vary and you should check in advance whether you will be asked to shoulder this additional cost.

Structural Survey

A thorough investigation of the structure of a property, preferably carried out by an independent qualified surveyor. There is no standard scale of fees for a structural survey.

Taxable Income

Income which is subjectable to tax and must be included when calculating your tax bill. It covers earnings from a job, income from self-employment, statutory sick pay, certain National Insurance benefits, unemployment related benefits, pensions, rental income, bank interest, building society interest and dividends.

Title Deeds

Documents which prove ownership of a freehold or leasehold

property. Usually this includes deeds detailing transfer of ownership over the previous decade or more as well as any mortgage deeds. If the title is registered a land certificate takes the place of the title deeds.

Top-Up Loans
An additional loan on top of an existing line of credit. Often used to describe a loan used to finance a home extension when the customer already has a mortgage on the property.

Transfer Deed
If you wish to sell your shares then you must sign a transfer deed. This only applies to registered stock and enables the company register to be kept up to date.

Under Offer
In England, Wales and Northern Ireland potential purchasers of a property can make an offer subject to survey. They are not legally bound by this offer until contracts have been exchanged. In Scotland, by contrast, an offer is legally binding.

Underinsurance
When the amount of insurance taken out is less than the full value of the property insured. If a claim is made on an underinsured property, the eventual payout may be reduced to mirror the degree of underinsurance.

Underwriting
The process of deciding whether a proposal can be accepted for insurance, what premium to charge and whether to apply any special terms.

Valuation
This is carried out by a qualified inspector on behalf of the building society or bank considering lending you the money to buy the property. You will foot the bill for this visit. It is important to distinguish between a valuation and a survey. A survey identifies structural faults as well as highlighting minor defects which may need attention at a later date. A valuation is an assessment of current value. It also describes the highly

technical process of how a life assurance company assesses the amount of how much money it may need to meet potential claims.

Vendor
The seller of a property.

Warranty
A stipulation attached to an insurance policy that the policyholder must meet. For example, a home contents policy might state that a burglar alarm should be installed and used. If the warranty is ignored, then any future claim arising may be refused.

Water Rates
An additional rate raised to cover the provision of water supply. It is based on the rateable value of the property and not at present related to the amount of water consumed.

With-Profits Endowment Mortgage
The sum assured is equal to the mortgage loan but any bonuses will be given to the borrower after the loan has been repaid. This is rather an expensive method of funding a mortgage, especially for first time borrowers who may have mortgaged themselves to the hilt at the outset.

With-Profits Policies
Life assurance policies that participate in the profits of the insurance company. The profits are attached to the policies in the form of bonuses.